READER'S THEATER
for Real-Life Mysteries

Author
Christina Hill, M.A.

Editor
Sara Connolly

Editor in Chief
Brent L. Fox, M. Ed.

Creative Director
Sarah M. Fournier

Cover Artist
Diem Pascarella

Illustrator
Renée Mc Elwee

Imaging
Amanda R. Harter

Publisher
Mary D. Smith, M.S. Ed.

Teacher Created Resources
12621 Western Avenue
Garden Grove, CA 92841
www.teachercreated.com

ISBN: 978-1-4206-1701-6

©2022 Teacher Created Resources

Made in U.S.A.

For standards correlations, visit
http://www.teachercreated.com/standards/

Table of Contents

Introduction

Are UFOs real? Why have so many ships and planes disappeared in the Bermuda Triangle? How could a human travel 9,000 miles in seconds without even realizing it? Real-life mysteries like these are a source of fascination for adults and children alike. These mysteries challenge our view of the world and can open our minds to new possibilities. In this book, real-life mysteries are presented in reader's theater format for an engaging activity that the whole class will love.

Research strongly indicates that reading text with fluency leads to student success in a variety of subject matters. Fluency is the ability to read a text with the appropriate speed, intonation, accuracy, and expression. Common Core literacy standards require students to "read grade-level text orally with accuracy, appropriate rate, and expression on successive readings." However, teachers and parents may struggle with finding ways to evaluate this level of fluency in their young readers. Simply reading and rereading to increase fluency may feel forced and might not provide students with the proper tools needed for reading comprehension. Additionally, not every young reader feels comfortable reading aloud. Shy students or struggling readers may dread oral reading or feel anxious about standing on a stage. Memorizing lines can also be stressful and intimidating to younger students. So, what is the solution? Cue *Reader's Theater for Real-Life Mysteries*!

Although repeated reading of a text is one of the best ways for a student to master fluency, no one wants to read the same text over and over *unless* it is something truly engaging! Reader's theater gives young readers the opportunity to embrace both oral reading and repeated readings in an exciting and fun way. The plays in this book offer fictional retellings of dramatic real-life unsolved mysteries. The drama and intrigue of the stories will hook the reader and the audience into these exciting mysteries. Students will learn to work together as a team as they perfect their lines for the culminating project—performing the play for parents, other students, or even a recorded online stream.

You may be wondering why reader's theater is not performed more often in the classroom. Some teachers worry that it will take up too much time or require too much work to present a successful performance. *Reader's Theater for Real-Life Mysteries* is designed to be simple and seamless. There are no props or costumes required. Each easy-to-follow lesson plan includes historical background content, vocabulary activities, and a culminating activity and journal page. Your student will be practicing reading fluency and building reading comprehension skills all while having fun!

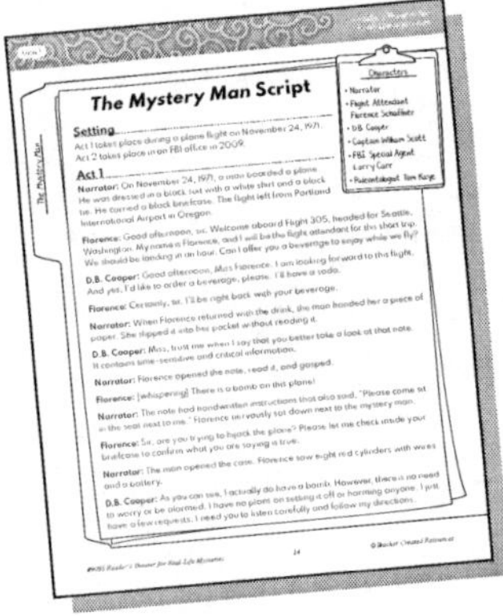

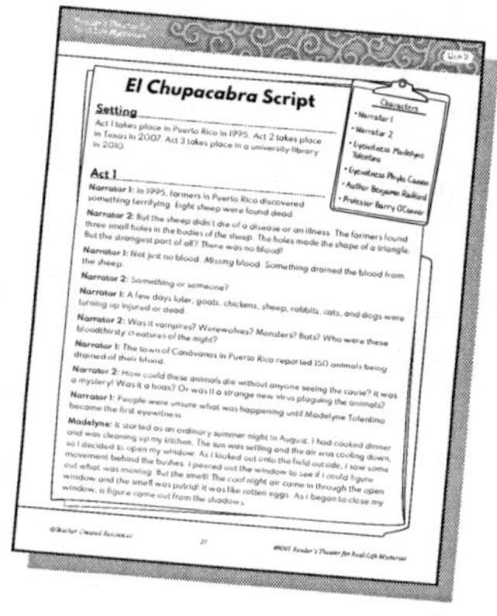

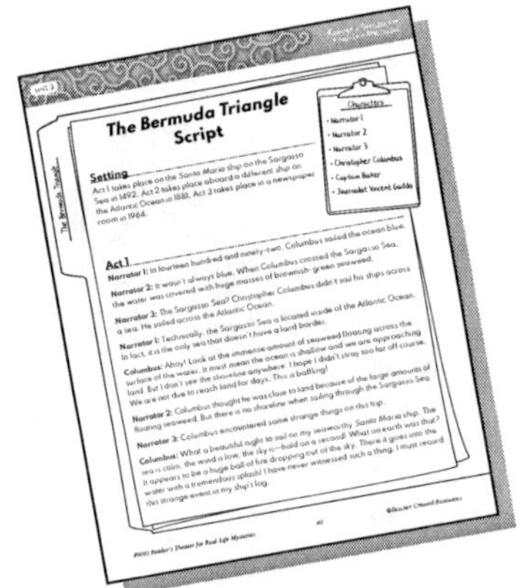

How to Use This Book

Reader's Theater for Real-Life Mysteries offers eight engaging scripts designed to be used with small groups of six students. Each play is divided into higher-level reading parts and lower-level reading parts. (This information is provided on the *Characters* page for each unit.) The roles in each script are listed from highest-reading level (high fifth grade) to lowest (high third grade). Note that the *Characters* page is provided as a teacher-only page so that you can distribute the roles according to students' reading abilities. Although the roles are differentiated, the students will not know which parts are harder than others. This gives everyone an equal chance to shine! If you have fewer than six students, you can offer a strong reader the chance to play two different roles at once. You can also consider performing the script more than once and having students play different roles each time!

Each lesson includes a short background description of the real-life mystery and some potential theories offered over time. Review this information before distributing the script, and discuss the background information with students. Each play is a fictional retelling of a real-life event. While dialogue and creative liberties were taken in writing the script, most of the characters are based on real people, and—more importantly—the events actually did happen. All eight mysteries are still considered unsolved.

Key vocabulary words are provided on the lesson plan pages. Consider frontloading the words with students before practicing the scripts to ensure that they understand these higher-level content words.

The best part about reader's theater is the simplicity! No stage, props, or costumes are required. However, if students are passionate about providing these elements, feel free to let them run with it.

Badges that students can decorate are provided for each character. There are various ways to use these badges:

- Make headbands out of construction paper, and staple the badges to them for students to wear.
- Pin the badges to students' shirts.
- Tape the badges to rulers, and have students hold them up while reading.
- Tie the badges to yarn, and have students wear them as necklaces.
- If students will be sitting in chairs, tape the badges to the wall above their heads.

How to Use This Book *(cont.)*

Provide each student with at least one copy of the script. (**Note:** If preferred, an additional copy of the script can be given to each student so they can practice reading at home.) Tell students to highlight their parts of the script so they do not miss their lines. Then practice, practice, practice! Give students silent-reading time so that they feel comfortable with their own parts before arranging them in small groups for oral reading practice.

While an actual performance is not required, the culminating performance day is something that students may look forward to the most. Consider having small groups perform for the whole class, or invite other classes to watch. A performance day where parents are invited to be the audience may be fun for students and a great way to connect home and school learning. Be sure to record the performance and share the video with parents. Another option is to do the whole performance as a livestream online. See page 8 for more information on online performances.

Once students have mastered their parts with fluency, you can assess their reading comprehension. The activity sheet offers comprehension questions and provides students with a self-assessment rubric. Review the self-assessment rubric so students understand how they will be scoring their performance. Students will benefit if they have the chance to listen to their own performance. See pages 7–8 for more information on recording performances.

After students have practiced and performed the reader's theater, you can conclude the unit with a writing activity. The final journal page provides students with the opportunity to express their own ideas and theories about what really happened during these mysterious moments in history!

Note: The reader's theater plays in this book are fictional retellings of real-life events. They were drawn from published materials and interviews. For narrative purposes, the stories contain fictionalized scenes and dialogue. The views, opinions, and dialogue belong to the characters only and may not be true representations of the views, opinions, and dialogue held or spoken by the real-life individuals.

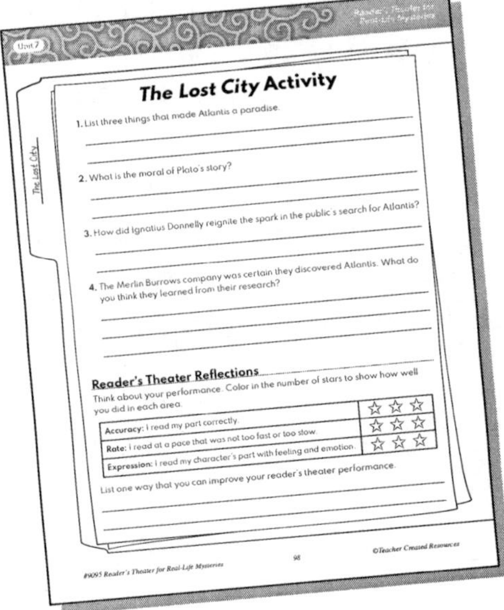

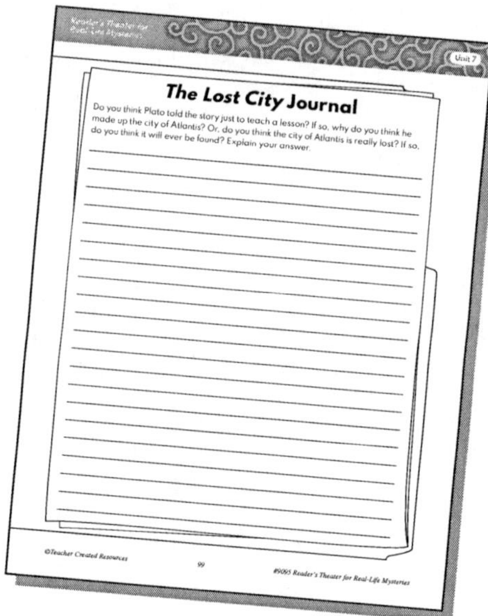

Hints for the Director

Take a deep breath. Being the director may seem intimidating for a theater production, but not for reader's theater! You will be pleasantly surprised at how little effort it takes to create a fun and engaging theater performance. Here are some tips to help you direct your readers into producing a successful performance:

- Do not feel pressed for time. It may seem daunting and impossible to fit a reader's theater play into an already tight classroom schedule. Carve out time whenever possible. All it takes is a few minutes a day for students to practice reading their parts. If you find yourself wrapping up class ten minutes early one day, tell students to pull out their scripts. You can also have the scripts be part of a language arts center or silent-reading time.

- Reading for fluency is a Common Core standard. Instead of viewing the performance as an extra task, simply build it into your language arts block and feel confident that students are meeting that standard in a fun and engaging way.

- Reader's theater is a collaborative project. Not only will your students be learning to read with fluency, but they will also be learning to work together as a team. Encourage students to support one another in this process. Strong readers can serve as mentors or coaches to struggling readers and help guide them on their path to fluency.

- Remind students that the goal is *not* memorization! Reader's theater is about reading. The goal is to read their lines with expression, confidence, and accuracy. They need to pay attention to punctuation and pause accordingly. They should speak in a loud enough voice for everyone to hear them. They should use proper inflection and speed when reading their parts.

- Meet one-on-one with each student at least once. Echo reading is a great way to teach fluency. Read the student's line out loud to them first, modeling correct inflection, intonation, speed, and expression. Then, have the student repeat the lines back to you. This will also be an opportunity for you to assess whether each student knows how to read and understand each word in their part.

- Make sure students have access to their highlighted scripts at all times. Consider having students create construction-paper covers to protect their scripts. If you have extra plastic folders, you can hole-punch their scripts and keep them in folders for protection.

Hints for the Director *(cont.)*

- Review basic theater rules with your students. Remind them to be still and extra quiet when it is not their turn to read. This will ensure that each student's part is heard. If they stumble over a word or make a mistake, the show must go on! Tell students to relax and do their best.

- Have students follow along the entire time the play is being performed. Listening is an important part of a reader's theater performance. If they do not follow along, they will miss their turn!

- If you find that your readers are struggling with knowing when it is their turn to speak, assign a student to be the director's assistant. If there is a pause during the play and no one knows whose turn it is, the assistant will quietly nod or make eye contact with the person who should be reading.

- Self-assessment is an important part of understanding fluency. Have students record their parts using Flipgrid, Seesaw, or any other video recording app your classroom uses. Then, have each student watch their own performance. Have them take notes about ways they can improve their own fluency. Did they mumble? Was there a line they stumbled over? Were they loud enough? Did they read too fast or too slow?

- Remember that no stage is required. Your production can be just a line of chairs at the front of the classroom or set in a small group circle.

- If you invited parents to come to the classroom, students can create playbills for them. They can create a backdrop for their play or decorate the classroom in any way that fits the script. If you have multiple small groups performing different scripts, you can have each group create a banner with the title of the play to hang behind their group. Props are not needed, and remember that students will need to hold their scripts. This will limit the use of any props.

- Don't forget to tell students to have fun! This is their chance to give it their all and show off their reading and acting skills. Embrace the timeless quality of theater production, and break a leg!

Tips for Online Reader's Theater

Reader's theater is easily adaptable to distance-learning groups using Zoom, Google Meet, Skype, or whichever video-conferencing software your school uses. If you are teaching a distance-learning group, provide each student with a copy of the script. They can highlight their parts either on a printed copy or an electronic one. You can follow the lesson plan the same way you would in the classroom. Provide students with time to practice their lines individually. You can also schedule a one-on-one meeting with each student to listen to them read their individual parts with fluency and to ensure that they understand their lines. Then, assign breakout rooms of small groups in Zoom or Skype so students can practice the script together. Consider allowing students to change their Zoom names to match their roles in the play. Once students feel comfortable reading their parts with fluency, designate a final performance day.

While distance or online learning presents challenges to some forms of instruction, it will not be a problem for reader's theater. In fact, you can work with teachers and students from anywhere in the world. Consider pairing up with another school to perform the play. Or, if your students have international penpals, you could perform a reader's theater with them! You can invite classes from another school to be part of the audience as well.

If your classroom uses Zoom or Google Meet, you can send out invites to parents to join the session and watch their children perform the reader's theater "live." As with any video conference, create a passcode to join the meeting. This will keep your session safe. Make sure students understand that during the live video conference, they need to be focused and quiet unless it is their turn to speak. A livestream online will be just like a real-life performance, and students will not have the option to stop or start over. Go over the same expectations and rules of theater with students that you would if they were performing in person.

If a livestream online performance does not work for scheduling purposes, or your students are worried about making mistakes, or even if you question the reliability of the internet connection, consider prerecording the performance instead. If you record the performance, students may feel more comfortable knowing that they can start over if they make a mistake. Just remind students that no performance is perfect, and part of theater is just rolling with the mistakes!

When recording a performance on Zoom (or whichever software you choose), you will typically be given an .MP4 file at the end. This is perfect for uploading to YouTube and sharing the link with parents to watch on their own viewing schedule. (Ensure that everything you post online is private and only accessible with the link you provide to students and parents.) You can also choose to drop it into a video-editing program, such as iMovie, and have students assist you with post-production video editing. Make sure students have access to watch the final performance video. This will help them with their self-assessment rubrics at the end of each unit.

The Mystery Man Lesson Plan

Content Objectives

- Read grade-level text orally with accuracy, appropriate rate, and expression on successive readings.
- Use knowledge of language and its conventions when writing, speaking, reading, or listening.
- Acknowledge differences in the points of view of characters, including by speaking in a different voice for each character when reading dialogue aloud.

Materials

- student copies of *The Mystery Man* Badge Art (pages 12–13)
- student copies of *The Mystery Man* Script (pages 14–19)
- student copies of *The Mystery Man* Activity (page 20)
- student copies of *The Mystery Man* Journal (page 21)
- highlighters, crayons, markers

Before Reading

1. Begin by assessing students' prior knowledge (if any) of the D.B. Cooper case. He has been a subject of pop culture for years and was even referenced in a recent superhero TV show. Tell students that on November 24, 1971, a man boarded a plane in Oregon. He bought a plane ticket using the name "Dan Cooper." He slipped a note to the flight attendant that said he had a bomb. He then had the FBI agree to his demands of $200,000 and four parachutes. The plane landed in Seattle, and the passengers were let off. The plane refueled and then headed toward Mexico with just the flight crew in the cockpit. Cooper was alone in the back of the empty plane. The pilot landed the plane to refuel in Nevada. The back exit hatch was open with the exit stairs lowered, and Cooper, the money, the parachutes, and the bomb were gone. This case has been studied and analyzed for years, and all that is known is that the mystery man was not really named Dan Cooper and his whereabouts are still unknown.

2. Ask students if anyone has been on an airplane. Allow them to share their experiences. Then, remind students that security at airports was very different in the 1970s. Passengers did not have to go through security points, have their bags checked, or even show identification to board a plane. Today, there are safety measures in place to prevent airplane hijackings.

3. Tell students that they will be performing a reader's theater play about the unsolved mystery of what happened to D.B. Cooper, the man who hijacked a plane and parachuted into the Pacific Northwest. Distribute copies of the script. Assign students their roles based on reading proficiencies. See page 11 for a list of the reading levels for each role in *The Mystery Man* script.

The Mystery Man Lesson Plan *(cont.)*

Rehearsal

1. Once students have been assigned their parts, tell them to go through the entire script and highlight their parts. Then, give students time to silently read either the entire script or just their highlighted sections. Ask them to use pencils to underline any words that they do not know or do not know how to pronounce. Go over these words together to ensure understanding.

2. This script has key vocabulary that students may not know. For a fun vocabulary twist, write each of the following words on a separate piece of paper: *hijack, currency, cockpit, aerospace, algae, serial numbers.* Hand each student one of the papers. Tell them to fold it into their best paper airplane! Then, have students take turns sailing the vocab-word paper airplanes to partners. The partner will unfold it, read the word, and look up the definition. Then, they can read the definition out loud and fly the next vocab-word paper airplane. Repeat until all the words have been defined and understood.

3. Give students time to practice their reader's theater. Remind them to speak with fluency, rate, expression, and tone. They need to play the role of the character using just their voices! Demonstrate reading a few lines in a dull, monotonous tone. Then, read the same lines with expression and ask students to explain the difference. Do the same thing with reading pace (read lines too quickly or too slowly), and then demonstrate a proper pace. Lastly, whisper lines softly. Then, read them again with a proper volume. Ask students if they understand the differences.

Performance

1. There are a variety of ways for your students to perform *The Mystery Man* reader's theater. See pages 5–8 for performance ideas.

2. Distribute copies of the badges (pages 12–13). Give students time to decorate their character's badge using crayons or markers.

3. Remind students to speak loudly and clearly and with confidence! Encourage them to show emotion and feeling with their voices. Even the narrator can show emotion by reading their part with an authoritative and confident tone! If stage fright or public speaking is an issue for some students, remind them to focus on their lines instead of worrying about the audience. And finally, remind students to take deep breaths, smile, and have fun!

Assessment

1. Distribute student copies of *The Mystery Man* Activity (page 20). Go over the activity sheet together and then have students complete it independently.

2. Distribute student copies of *The Mystery Man* Journal (page 21). Remind students that the story of D.B. Cooper is still an unsolved mystery. Discuss the possible theories presented in the script, along with any of your own. Then, give students time to journal their theories.

The Mystery Man Characters

Assigning Characters

The roles in this reader's theater have been leveled to fit the individual needs of your students. When students feel confident in their reading fluency, they will engage with the character and feel comfortable performing in front of others. The goal is to have a successful performance that allows each student a chance to shine.

The Mystery Man has six roles. Each role has been designed to meet the needs of a variety of reading-level proficiencies. The characters are listed here in order of highest reading-level proficiency to lowest.

Remember that even high-level readers may struggle with giving a fluent performance. Remind students that they are performing a play using only their voices. The way they speak each word matters! Demonstrate the difference between monotone reading and reading with fluency and expression so students can understand the expectations.

You might also consider assigning nonspeaking roles to students who are reluctant to read aloud. These students could act as directors or coaches. Remind them that their role is very important. They will have to know the script extremely well and will be in charge of prompting students when it is their turn to read.

Grade 5 Reading Levels:

Narrator Played by: ________________________

Paleontologist Tom Kaye Played by: ________________________

FBI Special Agent Larry Carr Played by: ________________________

Grade 4/High Grade 3 Reading Levels:

Captain William Scott Played by: ________________________

Flight Attendant Florence Schaffner Played by: ________________________

D.B. Cooper Played by: ________________________

The Mystery Man Badge Art

The Mystery Man Badge Art (cont.)

The Mystery Man Script

Characters
- Narrator
- Flight Attendant Florence Schaffner
- D.B. Cooper
- Captain William Scott
- FBI Special Agent Larry Carr
- Paleontologist Tom Kaye

Setting

Act 1 takes place during a plane flight on November 24, 1971. Act 2 takes place in an FBI office in 2009.

Act 1

Narrator: On November 24, 1971, a man boarded a plane. He was dressed in a black suit with a white shirt and a black tie. He carried a black briefcase. The flight left from Portland International Airport in Oregon.

Florence: Good afternoon, sir. Welcome aboard Flight 305, headed for Seattle, Washington. My name is Florence, and I will be the flight attendant for this short trip. We should be landing in an hour. Can I offer you a beverage to enjoy while we fly?

D.B. Cooper: Good afternoon, Miss Florence. I am looking forward to this flight. And yes, I'd like to order a beverage, please. I'll have a soda.

Florence: Certainly, sir. I'll be right back with your beverage.

Narrator: When Florence returned with the drink, the man handed her a piece of paper. She slipped it into her pocket without reading it.

D.B. Cooper: Miss, trust me when I say that you better take a look at that note. It contains time-sensitive and critical information.

Narrator: Florence opened the note, read it, and gasped.

Florence: [*whispering*] There is a bomb on this plane!

Narrator: The note had handwritten instructions that also said, "Please come sit in the seat next to me." Florence nervously sat down next to the mystery man.

Florence: Sir, are you trying to hijack the plane? Please let me check inside your briefcase to confirm what you are saying is true.

Narrator: The man opened the case. Florence saw eight red cylinders with wires and a battery.

D.B. Cooper: As you can see, I actually do have a bomb. However, there is no need to worry or be alarmed. I have no plans on setting it off or harming anyone. I just have a few requests. I need you to listen carefully and follow my directions.

The Mystery Man Script *(cont.)*

Florence: [*exhales loudly*] It is my job to keep everyone on this plane safe, so I am not sure I can help you. What exactly do you want?

D.B. Cooper: I want two hundred thousand dollars in American currency. Twenty-dollar bills are preferred. I also need four parachutes. Finally, please tell the pilot that we will need a fuel truck waiting at the airport to refill the tank. Oh, and ask them to send meals for the flight crew if they're hungry.

Florence: Sir, I have no idea if any of that is possible, but I'll speak with our pilot, Captain William Scott.

Narrator: Florence hurried to the cockpit of the plane.

Florence: Captain Scott, we have a situation! There is a man who is attempting to hijack the plane! He has a list of demands that he wants you to give him. I looked inside his briefcase, and it does appear to contain some kind of explosive device.

Captain Scott: Oh no! Do you think the passengers are in danger?

Florence: Actually, no. I think our plane is still safe. This mystery man is calm and polite and said he doesn't want to cause any harm. I believe him. But he is asking for a tremendous amount of money and four parachutes. How are we going to meet his requests?

Captain Scott: I will contact the air traffic controllers at Seattle airport. They can notify the FBI.

Florence: Oh my goodness! The FBI? Do you think they will be able to meet his outrageous demands? Two hundred thousand dollars is a huge amount of money!

Captain Scott: Don't worry, Florence. They will help us through this. Tell the man that we will meet his demands. Don't tell anyone except the other crew members what is happening. We need to keep everyone calm. Continue to do your job as usual. I will make the call.

Narrator: Florence returned to the passengers as the pilot called air-traffic control.

Captain Scott: Hello, can you hear me? This is Captain William Scott on Flight 305 heading for Seattle. Our plane has been hijacked. A man is demanding four parachutes and two hundred thousand dollars. I can circle the airport until you can collect what he needs. I will tell the passengers that we are having a minor mechanical problem.

The Mystery Man Script *(cont.)*

Florence: Sir, the pilot is arranging everything. We would like to keep this quiet in order to not create a panic among the other passengers. Is there anything else you need?

D.B. Cooper: No worries, Florence. I have no desire to cause a commotion. We can keep this whole operation a secret. As for anything else I need, I'd just like to order one more beverage, please. Oh, and I need to pay my bill.

Narrator: Florence served the mystery man one more drink. He paid his bill and told her to keep the change.

Captain Scott: Hello, passengers of Flight 305. We had a minor mechanical issue which has kept us circling the airport for a bit. It has been fixed. We apologize for the delay, and we will be landing shortly.

Narrator: The plane landed safely. The airline manager approached the back of the plane, and the stairs were extended down. Florence walked down the stairs. The airline manager handed the parachutes and the money to her. She climbed back onto the plane and gave everything to the mystery man.

D.B. Cooper: Thank you! Now, please instruct the pilot to refuel this plane for our next flight. I need him to fly south toward Mexico. But, he needs to fly slowly and at a lower altitude.

Narrator: Florence left the mystery man and returned to speak with the pilot.

Captain Scott: He has his parachutes and money. Now what is the plan?

Florence: He wants you to fly low and slow to Mexico. Is that even possible? Do you think he is going to try to jump out?

Captain Scott: That seems extremely dangerous. Also, this plane will not make it all the way to Mexico in one trip. Tell him I will need to land and refuel at the Reno Airport in Nevada.

Narrator: Florence relayed the message. The man agreed to the captain's plans.

Florence: Sir, what do you plan on doing? It is November and the middle of winter. There is a massive storm and it is freezing. If you jump, the odds of your survival are tremendously slim. And if you do survive, where will you go? You know the FBI will be looking for you.

The Mystery Man Script *(cont.)*

D.B. Cooper: Don't worry about me. I have my own plan. Thank you for all of your assistance. Please help the passengers get safely off the plane and stay with them. I will only need the flight crew in the cockpit to remain.

Narrator: Florence breathed a sigh of relief and exited the plane with the rest of the passengers. Then, the plane took off at 7:40 p.m. The rest of the flight crew stayed at the front of the plane and left the mystery man alone in the back. The police sent two fighter jets to follow, but they struggled to fly at such a slow speed. At 8:00 p.m., a warning light flashed in the cockpit.

Captain Scott: Hello, air traffic control? This is Captain Scott. We are still on course to land in Reno. I am calling to inform you that the hijacker opened the back door of the plane and lowered the exit stairs. I only know this because a warning light flashed. He instructed us to stay in the cockpit, so I am not sure if he jumped or not. I will have to land the plane with the stairs still lowered, but I think I can manage it safely.

Narrator: Captain Scott safely landed the plane at 10:15 p.m. The FBI searched the plane. The mystery man was gone! The briefcase, money, and two out of the four parachutes were also gone. The only item that remained was the black tie that the man had been wearing.

Captain Scott: What a strange day. I'm glad everyone is safe. As for the mystery man, I have no idea how he could have survived that jump. Our flight path was right over a dense forest on a dark and stormy night. The parachute he was wearing was not one he could steer. He must have known the area really well. He seemed to know everything about the flight path and even how this airplane operated. Who was he?

Act 2

Narrator: It's now 2009. The case of the mysterious hijacker remains unsolved. FBI Special Agent Larry Carr takes over the case. The FBI decides to team up with a paleontologist named Tom Kaye. They think his scientific knowledge can help crack the case.

Agent Carr: Hello, Mr. Kaye. My name is Special Agent Larry Carr. I am here to discuss your scientific research on the D.B. Cooper case. We have struggled to find this mystery man for years. All we know is that he bought a plane ticket under the name Dan Cooper. And today, he is known as D.B. Cooper. But all we really know is that it probably was not his real name. The list of suspects has been investigated for so many years. But there is not enough evidence. We don't have any more clues. We're hoping that your knowledge will help us.

The Mystery Man Script *(cont.)*

Tom: Hello, Agent Carr. Well, to begin, we decided to study the only piece of evidence left on the plane, which was D.B. Cooper's tie. A piece of clothing is tricky to study because most people wash their clothes often. But ties are different! Ties are worn for longer periods without being washed. This means that there are more particles left on the fabric to study. We analyzed the tie using an electron microscope. This technology was not available back in the 1970s.

Agent Carr: Science has certainly changed the way the FBI solves cases. So, what did you find on the tie?

Tom: Well, we found a lot of things, like pollen and different elements that you would commonly find on clothing. But the most interesting thing was the amount of titanium we collected from the tie. This was definitely unusual!

Agent Carr: Oh wow! Titanium is a rare metal, especially in the 1970s. So, perhaps Cooper worked in a metal factory of some sort.

Tom: Correct! I think he was an engineer in the aerospace industry. Those workers would have access to titanium.

Agent Carr: He seemed to know a lot about airplanes and how they function. I bet he was a manager or an engineer at an aerospace company. That explains why he was wearing a business suit too. I am going to start investigating those companies to see if anyone went missing at that time. What else have you discovered?

Tom: Well, let's talk about the money.

Narrator: In 1980, a young boy dug up three bundles of cash underneath the sand by the Columbia River. The amount of cash totaled five thousand, eight hundred dollars. The serial numbers on the bills matched those given to Cooper by the FBI.

Agent Carr: The money is the most puzzling part of this whole case! Many people believed that Cooper did not survive the jump. But we never found any evidence of that. The suitcase, parachutes, and Cooper himself have never turned up. The buried money was only a small part of what he received from the FBI. It seems strange that only part of the money was found. This leads people to believe that he really did survive the jump.

The Mystery Man Script *(cont.)*

Tom: Exactly. The buried money is such a mystery! I can't offer an explanation as to how the money got there, but I can provide some scientific evidence. To begin, we tried re-creating the event. We analyzed how a bundle of money would decay in the river water. We also studied the way the cash was found stacked. It is possible that the money traveled down the river and was buried under the sand naturally.

Agent Carr: That seems possible, especially because the money was found a pretty good distance away from the flight path.

Tom: True. But the more we studied the money, the more questions we had. There were ten bills missing from one of the stacks. Also, if the money floated down the river, it is highly unlikely that the three bundles would be buried under sand in the same spot. And finally, the rubber bands! There is no way the rubber bands would remain after years in the water. So that means the money had to wash up on the shore within a few years after Cooper jumped.

Agent Carr: Well, that is a possibility, right?

Tom: At this point, anything is possible. But we also found a type of algae on the surface of the money, and it only blooms in the springtime. This means that the money didn't enter the water in November when the hijacking occurred. The money needed to be buried months after the hijacking to have those algae particles. While this doesn't offer an explanation, it points to the idea that someone probably buried the money there. It could have been Cooper. But it isn't certain.

Agent Carr: We have made the serial numbers on the bills available to the public in order to help find more missing bills. But it has been years and these stacks were the only ones ever found. Who was D.B. Cooper? And what was he trying to do? I am determined to solve this puzzling case!

Narrator: Even today, the mystery man has not been found. In 2016, the FBI closed the case and left it unsolved. However, there are hundreds of theories about who D.B. Cooper was and what happened to him. Was he a spy for a foreign country? Or perhaps a crime-fighting superhero? Did he even survive the jump? Why did he need the money if he wasn't going to spend it? Was he a time traveler? Did he jump out of the plane and into a different dimension? What do *you* think happened?

The Mystery Man Activity

1. What does the word *aerospace* mean?

____

____

2. Why did the FBI make the serial numbers of the bills public?

____

____

3. How has technology changed the way the FBI investigates cases? __________

____

____

4. Why did the buried money add to the mystery of this case? ______________

____

____

____

Reader's Theater Reflections

Think about your performance. Color in the number of stars to show how well you did in each area.

Accuracy: I read my part correctly.	☆ ☆ ☆
Rate: I read at a pace that was not too fast or too slow.	☆ ☆ ☆
Expression: I read my character's part with feeling and emotion.	☆ ☆ ☆

List one way that you can improve your reader's theater performance.

____

____

The Mystery Man Journal

On November 24, 1971, D.B. Cooper disappeared from an airplane. Despite years of investigation, he was never found. This remains an unsolved mystery. What do you think happened to him? Why do you think he hijacked the plane?

El Chupacabra Lesson Plan

Content Objectives

- Read grade-level text orally with accuracy, appropriate rate, and expression on successive readings.
- Use knowledge of language and its conventions when writing, speaking, reading, or listening.
- Acknowledge differences in the points of view of characters, including by speaking in a different voice for each character when reading dialogue aloud.

Materials

- student copies of *El Chupacabra* Badge Art (pages 25–26)
- student copies of *El Chupacabra* Script (pages 27–32)
- student copies of *El Chupacabra* Activity (page 33)
- student copies of *El Chupacabra* Journal (page 34)
- highlighters, crayons, markers
- notecards and dice for vocabulary game

Before Reading

1. Begin by assessing students' prior knowledge (if any) of the mysterious chupacabra. They may have heard the name from folklore, books, or movies. The legend began in Puerto Rico when eight sheep were found with puncture marks in their bodies. They appeared to be drained of their blood. People thought it must be vampires. But then a woman claimed she saw a creature that looked like a dog but had no fur and hopped like a kangaroo. The town called the creature *el chupacabra*, which means "the goat sucker." The tales of the chupacabra spread across the world, and despite many attempts to solve the mystery, it remains mostly an enigma to this day.

2. Tell students that they will be performing a reader's theater play about the unsolved mystery of the chupacabra. Distribute copies of the script. Assign students their roles based on reading proficiencies. See page 24 for a list of the reading levels for each role in the *El Chupacabra* script.

El Chupacabra Lesson Plan *(cont.)*

Rehearsal

1. Once students have been assigned their parts, tell them to go through the entire script and highlight their parts. Then, give students time to silently read either the entire script or just their highlighted sections. Ask them to use a pencil and underline any words that they do not know or do not know how to pronounce. Go over these words together to ensure understanding.

2. This script has key vocabulary that students may not know. Consider playing a vocabulary game. Have students sit with partners. Write the following words from the play on note cards: *plaguing, putrid, quills, lurking, prowling, documentaries, compiling, figment, shapeshifter, arachnids.* Each student will take turns reading a word on a notecard. Then, they will give the definition. If they do not know, they can look it up. Then, they will roll the dice and write down the number they scored. Partners go back and forth until all ten words are defined. Then, they total their scores to see who wins!

3. Give students time to practice their reader's theater. Remind them to speak with fluency, rate, expression, and tone. They need to play the role of the character using just their voices! Demonstrate reading a few lines in a dull, monotonous tone. Then, read the same lines with expression and ask students to explain the difference. Do the same thing with reading pace (read lines too quickly or too slowly), and then demonstrate a proper pace. Finally, whisper lines softly. Then, read them again with a proper volume. Ask students if they understand the differences.

Performance

1. There are a variety of ways for your students to perform the *El Chupacabra* reader's theater. See pages 5–8 for performance ideas.

2. Distribute copies of the badges (pages 25–26). Give students time to decorate their character's badge using crayons or markers.

3. Remind students to speak loudly and clearly and with confidence! Encourage them to show emotion and feeling with their voices. Even the narrator can show emotion by reading their part with an authoritative and confident tone! If stage fright or public speaking is an issue for some students, remind them to focus on their lines instead of worrying about the audience. And finally, remind students to take deep breaths, smile, and have fun!

Assessment

1. Distribute student copies of the *El Chupacabra* Activity (page 33). Go over the activity sheet together, and then have students complete it independently.

2. Distribute student copies of the *El Chupacabra* Journal (page 34). Remind students that the existence of the chupacabra is still an unsolved mystery. Discuss the possible theories presented in the script, along with any of your own. Then, give students time to journal their theories.

El Chupacabra Characters

Assigning Characters

The roles in this reader's theater have been leveled to fit the individual needs of your students. When students feel confident in their reading fluency, they will engage with the character and feel comfortable performing in front of others. The goal is to have a successful performance that allows each student a chance to shine.

El Chupacabra has six roles. Each role has been designed to meet the needs of a variety of reading-level proficiencies. The characters are listed here in order of highest reading-level proficiency to lowest.

Remember that even high-level readers may struggle with giving a fluent performance. Remind students that they are performing a play using only their voices. The way they speak each word matters! Demonstrate the difference between monotone reading and reading with fluency and expression so students can understand the expectations.

You might also consider assigning nonspeaking roles to students who are reluctant to read aloud. These students could act as directors or coaches. Remind them that their role is very important. They will have to know the script extremely well and will be in charge of prompting students when it is their turn to read.

Grade 5 Reading Levels:

Narrator 1   Played by: _______________________________

Author Benjamin Radford   Played by: _______________________________

Professor Barry O'Connor   Played by: _______________________________

Grade 4/High Grade 3 Reading Levels:

Eyewitness Madelyne Tolentino Played by: _______________________________

Eyewitness Phylis Canion   Played by: _______________________________

Narrator 2   Played by: _______________________________

El Chupacabra Badge Art

El Chupacabra Badge Art (cont.)

El Chupacabra Script

Characters

- Narrator 1
- Narrator 2
- Eyewitness Madelyne Tolentino
- Eyewitness Phylis Canion
- Author Benjamin Radford
- Professor Barry O'Connor

Setting

Act 1 takes place in Puerto Rico in 1995. Act 2 takes place in Texas in 2007. Act 3 takes place in a university library in 2010.

Act 1

Narrator 1: In 1995, farmers in Puerto Rico discovered something terrifying. Eight sheep were found dead.

Narrator 2: But the sheep didn't die of a disease or an illness. The farmers found three small holes in the bodies of the sheep. The holes made the shape of a triangle. But the strangest part of all? There was no blood!

Narrator 1: Not just no blood. *Missing* blood. Something drained the blood from the sheep.

Narrator 2: Something or someone?

Narrator 1: A few days later, goats, chickens, sheep, rabbits, cats, and dogs were turning up injured or dead.

Narrator 2: Was it vampires? Werewolves? Monsters? Bats? Who were these bloodthirsty creatures of the night?

Narrator 1: The town of Canóvanas in Puerto Rico reported 150 animals being drained of their blood.

Narrator 2: How could these animals die without anyone seeing the cause? It was a mystery! Was it a hoax? Or was it a strange new virus plaguing the animals?

Narrator 1: People were unsure what was happening until Madelyne Tolentino became the first eyewitness.

Madelyne: It started as an ordinary summer night in August. I had cooked dinner and was cleaning up my kitchen. The sun was setting and the air was cooling down, so I decided to open my window. As I looked out onto the field outside, I saw some movement behind the bushes. I peered out the window to see if I could figure out what was moving. But the smell! The cool night air came in through the open window and the smell was putrid! It was like rotten eggs. As I began to close my window, a figure came out from the shadows.

El Chupacabra Script (cont.)

Narrator 2: [*whispering*] *El chupacabra.*

Madelyne: Its black eyes glistened in the moonlight. It was unlike anything I had ever seen before. At first, I thought it was a coyote or a wolf. But it was standing on two legs! It had spines down its back, kind of like quills. It had dark, scaly skin like a reptile. It did not have any fur or hair. I think it had a tail, but it was too dark to see clearly. I was trying to identify what kind of animal it could be. I guess it was almost like a small bear. But then it started to hop like a kangaroo! That is what spooked me the most! It looked unworldly. What if it was an alien? I had shivers run down my spine! I locked all my windows and doors just in case.

Narrator 2: [*whispering*] *El chupacabra.*

Narrator 1: *El chupa*-what?

Narrator 2: [*whispering*] *El chupacabra.*

Madelyne: I had heard stories of local farm animals turning up dead. I am certain this creature of the night is the one responsible. So the next day, I went to the police and told them what I saw. They had an artist sketch an illustration of it and published it in the local newspaper. I thought that no one would believe me. But people did! Other people came forward and said they saw similar creatures lurking around their yards. The locals around here began calling the creature *el chupacabra,* which translates to "goat sucker" in Spanish. But these creatures were not just in our town. Word spread and more reports claimed that these creatures were turning up in Mexico, Argentina, Chile, and Colombia.

Narrator 1: The creatures, or chupacabras, continued to attack. Or, at least that's what people claimed. No one actually saw a chupacabra commit a blood-sucking crime.

Narrator 2: Some people didn't believe the stories. They said it was just folklore or fantasy. But others were believers. They told tales of the things they saw. Or at least the things they *think* they saw.

Act 2

Narrator 1: Twelve years later, the legend of *el chupacabra* has spread to the United States.

El Chupacabra Script *(cont.)*

Narrator 2: Phylis Canion was working on her ranch in Texas. It was a hot summer day in June. She saw something strange outside. It was prowling in the fields behind her home.

Phylis: Oh my goodness! What in the world is that? Is that a dog? No, it looks more like a coyote. But where is its fur? It looks like a blue-gray hairless monster!

Narrator 1: Phylis didn't think much about the creature until she found one of the chickens on her ranch drained of its blood, with puncture marks on its body.

Phylis: [*whispering*] *El chupacabra.*

Narrator 2: Phylis was determined. She wanted to catch one of the creatures.

Phylis: I set up cameras across my property. I studied the footage for a few days but found nothing. But a few more of my chickens were killed, and I wasn't going to give up the hunt! So I decided to talk to some of my neighbors to make sure they were on alert. The legend of *el chupacabra* was known to all the folks who live in this part of Texas. We had stories of sightings, but nobody could prove anything. But then, a month later, my neighbor called me. He found an actual creature on the side of the road. It had been hit by a car.

Narrator 1: Phylis headed over to investigate.

Phylis: I couldn't believe my eyes! The creature was exactly like the one I saw walking across my pasture.

Narrator 2: [*whispering*] *El chupacabra.*

Phylis: It had a scrawny body and no hair or fur. Its skin was gray and its face was similar to a coyote. But something about it was definitely different. I have lived out here for years and have never seen this kind of animal. So with the help of my neighbor, we loaded the body into my tractor and I drove it home. I took photos of it and submitted them. And the world noticed!

Narrator 1: Phylis ended up a celebrity. She had the creature stuffed and put on display. Her story has been featured in a variety of documentaries.

Phylis: I have been on National Geographic, the History Channel, and even Animal Planet. People are fascinated with the history of the chupacabras because they are such strange and mythical creatures.

El Chupacabra Script *(cont.)*

Narrator 2: Some people had doubts. The creature looked like a coyote. But still, something about it was different. What happened to its fur? Would this mystery ever be solved?

Act 3

Narrator 1: Three years later, the investigations continued. Benjamin Radford is an author. He decided to write a book about the unsolved mystery of *el chupacabra*. He began by interviewing both Phylis and Madelyne.

Narrator 2: He also invited Barry O'Connor to join them. Barry O'Connor is a biologist. He has his own theories on the mysterious creatures.

Benjamin: Good afternoon, Phylis, Madelyne, and Barry. Thank you all so much for meeting me here. As you know, I have been researching the unsolved mystery of *el chupacabra* for many years and am compiling a book. I would love to hear your theories and ideas to help me in my investigation.

Madelyne: Well, it's been many years since I saw the creature, but I will do my best to remember.

Benjamin: Thank you, Madelyne. Let's start with your story. You were the first eyewitness, correct?

Madelyne: I am not sure I was the first eyewitness. *El chupacabra* has plagued my town for many years. I think I am just the first to report it and have an illustration rendered.

Benjamin: I studied the illustration. I was amused that it looks very similar to a creature I saw years ago in a science fiction movie. I looked it up and discovered that the movie came out the same year you saw the creature. I found this connection fascinating. By any chance did you watch the movie called *Species*?

Madelyne: Hmmm. Yes! I remember that movie well. Oh, you are right! The creature I saw did look so much like those aliens. That must be it! These creatures are aliens!

Benjamin: I wouldn't go so far as to say they are aliens. But maybe you remembered what you saw in the movie. Your mind can play tricks on you.

Madelyne: Benjamin, this creature is not a figment of my imagination.

El Chupacabra **Script** *(cont.)*

Benjamin: Oh, I believe you saw something. I am just trying to investigate exactly what it was that you saw. Let's move on to Phylis. I have seen the creature you found on the side of the road. It doesn't look like what Madelyne described at all.

Phylis: I thought that too. But maybe Texas has its own species of chupacabra.

Benjamin: That could be true. That is exactly why I am so interested in this topic. I feel like the concept of *el chupacabra* is vast and multi-layered. If I can solve each individual mystery, it will help me solve the bigger one. The descriptions of *el chupacabra* are as ordinary as dogs and bats and are as strange as monkeys, kangaroos, goblins, vampires, and aliens!

Phylis: Maybe it's a shapeshifter!

Benjamin: Barry, tell us what you think. I read that you have been studying these creatures for as long as I have.

Barry: Yes, indeed. Thank you for inviting me to speak with you. I have my own theories, although I am not sure they are as exciting as vampires or aliens. I do believe that all legends are based on something factual and true. You correctly pointed out that what Phylis saw in Texas is much different from what Madelyne saw in Puerto Rico. So instead of looking at the differences, I decided to study the similarities. Both creatures were believed to have killed livestock. Both creatures were described as smelly, and both creatures lacked hair or fur.

Benjamin: I like that approach. But clearly these creatures are not from outer space, right? Although I think it's human nature to want to believe in mythical monsters, especially ones that don't attack humans.

Barry: I agree with you. I do not think these creatures are alien at all. I think they are animals who are very sick with mange.

Benjamin: Mange? The skin disease?

Barry: Correct! Let me explain my research. Animals get mange because of mites, which are tiny arachnids. These mites burrow into an animal's skin, which causes all the animal's hair to fall out. Their skin also thickens and resembles that of a reptile. If the mange gets really bad, the entire body is infected. This causes a really stinky smell. It also distorts the animal's face and causes swelling.

El Chupacabra Script *(cont.)*

Phylis: I have seen dogs with mange, but they never look like this. And why are these creatures killing livestock?

Benjamin: Does the mange make them weaker? Maybe the livestock are easy targets?

Barry: That is a really great theory. The disease takes its toll on their bodies, making them unable to hunt for wild animals. It makes sense that they would attack goats and chickens that are easier to hunt.

Phylis: But I have dogs. They would never hunt livestock.

Barry: I agree. But I don't believe your chupacabras are regular dogs. Humans and domestic dogs are pretty safe from this level of infection. I think the creatures found in Texas might be coyotes that are severely infected with mange.

Madelyne: What about in my town? I can guarantee that I did not see a coyote.

Barry: I thought a lot about that too. I think that you saw a monkey with mange. That explains the walking on two legs part. And there are wild monkeys in Puerto Rico, right?

Madelyne: I suppose so. I still don't know if I am convinced. Why would mangy animals suck blood from livestock? They aren't vampires.

Benjamin: There are many questions left unanswered, and I am determined to get to the bottom of this. I am skeptical about the tall tales of vampires or alien creatures being responsible. I think I'm leaning towards Barry's theory of chupacabras being animals infected with mange.

Narrator 1: While there are still a number of theories circulating, there are still some lingering questions that leave this case an unsolved mystery. Who is the mysterious blood-sucking creature?

Narrator 2: [*whispering*] *El chupacabra.*

Narrator 1: Do chupacabras really exist? Or are they all just mangy animals? What do *you* think?

El Chupacabra Activity

1. How are the chupacabras in Puerto Rico different from the ones found in Texas?

____

____

2. What is *mange*?

____

____

3. Do you agree with Professor O'Connor's chupacabra theory? Why or why not?

____

____

4. Would you ever want to see a chupacabra? Why or why not?

____

____

____

Reader's Theater Reflections

Think about your performance. Color in the number of stars to show how well
you did in each area.

Accuracy: I read my part correctly.	☆ ☆ ☆
Rate: I read at a pace that was not too fast or too slow.	☆ ☆ ☆
Expression: I read my character's part with feeling and emotion.	☆ ☆ ☆

List one way that you can improve your reader's theater performance.

____

____

El Chupacabra Journal

Despite the many theories about *el chupacabra*, nothing is completely certain. It remains an unsolved mystery. Do you think the chupacabras are real? Are they vampires, aliens, or just mangy animals?

The Bermuda Triangle Lesson Plan

Content Objectives

- Read grade-level text orally with accuracy, appropriate rate, and expression on successive readings.
- Use knowledge of language and its conventions when writing, speaking, reading, or listening.
- Acknowledge differences in the points of view of characters, including by speaking in a different voice for each character when reading dialogue aloud.

Materials

- student copies of *The Bermuda Triangle* Badge Art (pages 38–39)
- student copies of *The Bermuda Triangle* Script (pages 40–45)
- student copies of *The Bermuda Triangle* Activity (page 46)
- student copies of *The Bermuda Triangle* Journal (page 47)
- highlighters, crayons, markers

Before Reading

1. Begin by assessing students' prior knowledge (if any) of the Bermuda Triangle. Explain to students that this is not an actual place found on a map. It is a term coined by a journalist to label the area in the Atlantic Ocean where mysterious things keep happening. If possible, show students a map of the Bermuda Triangle region. The three points of the triangle are Bermuda, Florida, and Puerto Rico. The storms across this area of the world are unpredictable and sudden. Many people think these environmental factors are the reason that boats and planes have disappeared without a trace. However, there are also many supernatural theories that include aliens, wormholes to other dimensions, and magnetic disturbances. The U.S. Coast Guard claims that it is a mix of strong forces of nature and human error that causes these ships and planes to disappear. But the tales of mystery started long ago and continue even to this day. Many of the events that have taken place in the Bermuda Triangle remain unsolved mysteries.

2. Tell students that they will be performing a reader's theater play about the unsolved mystery of the Bermuda Triangle. Distribute copies of the script. Assign students their roles based on reading proficiencies. See page 37 for a list of the reading levels for each role in *The Bermuda Triangle* script.

The Bermuda Triangle **Lesson Plan** (cont.)

Rehearsal

1. Once students have been assigned their parts, tell them to go through the entire script and highlight their parts. Then, give students time to silently read either the entire script or just their highlighted sections. Ask them to use a pencil and underline any words that they do not know or do not know how to pronounce. Go over these words together to ensure understanding.

2. This script has key vocabulary that students may not know. Consider playing a vocabulary game or creating a word wall. Write the following words from the play on the board or a piece of chart paper: *compass, port, variation, parallel universe, malfunctioning, treacherous, paranormal, decompose, wreckage.* Ask students to help you define each one. Write the definitions next to the words. If students are unsure of the definitions, have them read the dictionary definitions to you.

3. Give students time to practice their reader's theater. Remind them to speak with fluency, rate, expression, and tone. They need to play the role of the character using just their voices! Demonstrate reading a few lines in a dull, monotonous tone. Then, read the same lines with expression and ask students to explain the difference. Do the same thing with reading pace (read lines too quickly or too slowly), and then demonstrate a proper pace. Finally, whisper lines softly. Then, read them again with a proper volume. Ask students if they understand the differences.

Performance

1. There are a variety of ways for your students to perform *The Bermuda Triangle* reader's theater. See pages 5–8 for performance ideas.

2. Distribute copies of the badges (pages 38–39). Give students time to decorate their character's badge using crayons or markers.

3. Remind students to speak loudly and clearly and with confidence! Encourage them to show emotion and feeling with their voices. Even the narrator can show emotion by reading their part with an authoritative and confident tone! If stage fright or public speaking is an issue for some students, remind them to focus on their lines instead of worrying about the audience. And finally, remind students to take deep breaths, smile, and have fun!

Assessment

1. Distribute student copies of *The Bermuda Triangle* Activity (page 46). Go over the activity sheet together, and then have students complete it independently.

2. Distribute student copies of *The Bermuda Triangle* Journal (page 47). Remind students that the strange occurrences linked to the Bermuda Triangle are still unsolved mysteries. Discuss the possible theories presented in the script, along with any of your own. Then, give students time to journal their theories.

The Bermuda Triangle Characters

Assigning Characters

The roles in this reader's theater have been leveled to fit the individual needs of your students. When students feel confident in their reading fluency, they will engage with the character and feel comfortable performing in front of others. The goal is to have a successful performance that allows each student a chance to shine.

The Bermuda Triangle has six roles. Each role has been designed to meet the needs of a variety of reading-level proficiencies. The characters are listed here in order of highest reading-level proficiency to lowest.

Remember that even high-level readers may struggle with giving a fluent performance. Remind students that they are performing a play using only their voices. The way they speak each word matters! Demonstrate the difference between monotone reading and reading with fluency and expression so students can understand the expectations.

You might also consider assigning nonspeaking roles to students who are reluctant to read aloud. These students could act as directors or coaches. Remind them that their role is very important. They will have to know the script extremely well and will be in charge of prompting students when it is their turn to read.

Grade 5 Reading Levels:

Narrator 1   Played by: _______________________________

Narrator 2   Played by: _______________________________

Narrator 3   Played by: _______________________________

Grade 4/High Grade 3 Reading Levels:

Journalist Vincent Gaddis   Played by: _______________________________

Captain Baker   Played by: _______________________________

Christopher Columbus   Played by: _______________________________

The Bermuda Triangle Badge Art

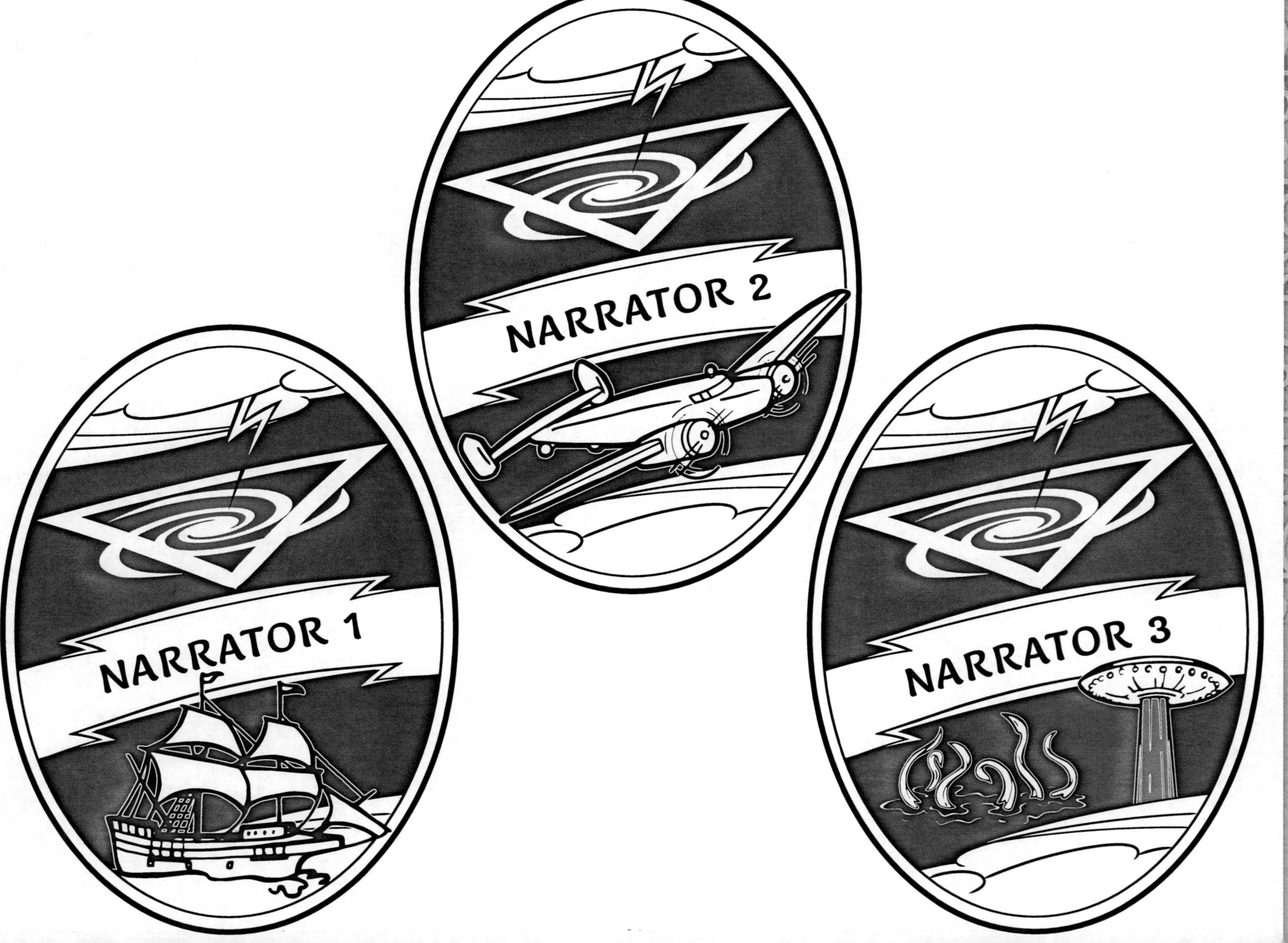

 38

The Bermuda Triangle Badge Art (cont.)

The Bermuda Triangle Script

Setting

Act 1 takes place on the *Santa Maria* ship on the Sargasso Sea in 1492. Act 2 takes place aboard a different ship on the Atlantic Ocean in 1881. Act 3 takes place in a newspaper room in 1964.

Characters
- Narrator 1
- Narrator 2
- Narrator 3
- Christopher Columbus
- Captain Baker
- Journalist Vincent Gaddis

Act 1

Narrator 1: In fourteen hundred and ninety-two, Columbus sailed the ocean blue.

Narrator 2: It wasn't always blue. When Columbus crossed the Sargasso Sea, the water was covered with huge masses of brownish-green seaweed.

Narrator 3: The Sargasso Sea? Christopher Columbus didn't sail his ships across a sea. He sailed across the Atlantic Ocean.

Narrator 1: Technically, the Sargasso Sea is located inside of the Atlantic Ocean. In fact, it is the only sea that doesn't have a land border.

Columbus: Ahoy! Look at the immense amount of seaweed floating across the surface of the water. It must mean the ocean is shallow and we are approaching land. But I don't see the shoreline anywhere. I hope I didn't stray too far off course. We are not due to reach land for days. This is baffling!

Narrator 2: Columbus thought he was close to land because of the large amounts of floating seaweed. But there is no shoreline when sailing through the Sargasso Sea.

Narrator 3: Columbus encountered some strange things on this trip.

Columbus: What a beautiful night to sail on my seaworthy *Santa Maria* ship. The sea is calm, the wind is low, the sky is—hold on a second! What on earth was that? It appears to be a huge ball of fire dropping out of the sky. There it goes into the water with a tremendous splash! I have never witnessed such a thing. I must record this strange event in my ship's log.

The Bermuda Triangle Script *(cont.)*

Narrator 3: The next day was just as strange. More unusual things happened.

Columbus: I am completely astounded! My compass does not seem to work. I have checked every compass on this ship. They are pointing north, but something seems off. I can't quite figure it out. I feel like every compass is leading me off my original course! It is quite puzzling. I have never had all of the compasses fail me! I hope we reach our destination.

Narrator 1: A compass is designed to point to magnetic north. This is different from true north. If you follow a compass north, it will not lead you to the North Pole. It will actually lead you 1,500 miles away in Canada.

Narrator 2: Columbus noticed that the north on his compass was shifting. This is unusual.

Narrator 3: This is called "compass variation."

Columbus: I must record the events in my log. This voyage just keeps getting stranger. After an entire day of my compass malfunctioning, I saw another odd sight. Last night it was a giant fireball falling from the sky. But tonight, I saw a candle flickering in the distance out on the water! The strangest part is that we are nowhere near the land. What could this light possibly be? This truly is a curious journey.

Narrator 1: Columbus and his crew made it safely through the strange sea.

Narrator 2: But the mysterious stories continued.

Act 2

Narrator 3: Tales of disappearing ships and mysterious sightings continued.

Narrator 1: In 1881, Captain Baker and his crew were sailing a ship called the *Ellen Austin*.

Narrator 2: They were sailing from London to New York.

Captain Baker: This is a peculiar night out here on the Atlantic Ocean. The water is so calm, and there is barely any wind. I have traveled this route before, and this area always feels eerie to me.

Narrator 3: Captain Baker spotted something out in the distance.

The Bermuda Triangle Script *(cont.)*

The Bermuda Triangle

Captain Baker: I wonder what that is. It looks like a ship, but it isn't sailing correctly. It appears to be drifting unsteadily. I will change course to see if they need assistance.

Narrator 1: Captain Baker steered the *Ellen Austin* toward the mysterious ship.

Narrator 2: He boarded the ship to see if the other captain needed help.

Captain Baker: How unusual! This ship is completely empty. It must be abandoned. There are no signs of a struggle of any kind. The nameplates have been removed, and the ship's log is missing. I have no way of knowing whose ship this is. I'll have a few of my crewmembers sail her to port.

Narrator 3: The crew sailed the mysterious ship next to the *Ellen Austin*. But they lost track of each other after a bad storm.

Narrator 1: But a few days later, Captain Baker saw the ship again.

Captain Baker: Ahoy! There they are! What a relief. I was worried that something had happened to them during that treacherous storm. Lucky for us, the sky stopped pouring rain and the sun is shining again. I'll steer my ship closer to see how their journey is coming along.

Narrator 2: But when Captain Baker got closer to the ship, he was bewildered.

Captain Baker: Why are they sailing so aimlessly? They don't even seem to be following our course.

Narrator 3: Captain Baker got close enough to board the mystery ship.

Captain Baker: This ship is abandoned. My crewmates have disappeared. But all of the food and supplies are still here. The only things missing are the crew and the new log book I left with them. It's happening again. Is this a cursed ghost ship?

Narrator 1: But Captain Baker was not completely convinced. He knew that if he could get the ship to port, he would be paid a large sum of money. He decided to send more of his crewmates to board the ship and have a second attempt at sailing to New York.

Captain Baker: Don't worry, fellow sailors. There is nothing to fear, and I am certain this was just a coincidence. Stay close to my ship, stay on course, and everything will be fine. We don't have too far left to go on this voyage.

The Bermuda Triangle Script *(cont.)*

Narrator 2: The two ships sailed closely for most of the journey. But then, a dense fog settled across the ocean.

Captain Baker: Curse this blasted fog! I can't see a thing. And the wind has left us barely moving. I am sure when it lifts, we will see their ship again.

Narrator 3: But Captain Baker was wrong. The fog lifted. The mysterious ghost ship was gone. It was never seen again.

Captain Baker: I have been an experienced sailor for many years, and I have no explanation for what happened out there on the Atlantic Ocean that day.

Act 3

Narrator 1: Over the years, tales of strange sightings and mysterious disappearances continued. The stories reached the public, and people began to worry.

Narrator 2: Vincent Gaddis is a journalist. He began to study the stories. He noticed something remarkable.

Vincent: So many of the mysteries occur in the same region of the Atlantic Ocean. I plotted the points out on a map. Connecting them forms a perfect triangle. The three points are Bermuda, Florida, and Puerto Rico. I think I will call it the Bermuda Triangle! There has to be a reason why so many strange happenings are located in this triangle. I am determined to solve the mystery! I am going to write about my ideas.

Narrator 3: In 1964, Gaddis began his research. He wanted to write an article. It was titled, "The Deadly Bermuda Triangle."

Vincent: I already knew the stories about Christopher Columbus and the mysterious ghost ship. But new events kept happening. In 1935, a group of five U.S. Navy planes left Florida together for a training exercise. They were known as Flight 19. One pilot radioed that they were lost. His compass wasn't working. The navy sent a rescue plane to look for them. When he didn't return, they radioed him. But all they got in return was silence. None of the six planes were ever seen again.

Narrator 1: People thought the planes all crashed into the ocean. But no wreckage was ever found.

Narrator 2: The navy issued a report stating that the planes disappeared as if they had flown to Mars.

The Bermuda Triangle Script *(cont.)*

Vincent: In 1948, a large passenger plane called the *Star Tiger* was flying to Bermuda. There was no distress call. The plane was full of fuel. The flight crew was experienced. They just completely vanished! What's even stranger is that one year later, another large airliner disappeared. It was called the *Star Ariel*. It was also flying over the Bermuda Triangle.

Narrator 3: The disappearances were also happening in the water.

Vincent: Just like the planes, there were a series of lost ships reported. In 1918, a giant cargo ship set sail. It was called the USS *Cyclops*. It was carrying 300 passengers across the Bermuda Triangle. The last radio call was, "weather fair, all well." The entire ship vanished and was never seen again.

Narrator 1: How could a giant cargo ship vanish? Why was there no distress call? Despite attempts at searching the sea for wreckage, nothing was ever found.

Vincent: In 1941, two more navy ships vanished along the same route. There are too many coincidences to count! There must be a reason for it all.

Narrator 2: Vincent researched the possible theories.

Vincent: The most common theory is the weather. The Gulf Stream that runs through this area can cause massive storms. The area is also known for waterspouts, which are tornadoes that form on the water. There are earthquakes that can cause large waves. These rogue waves can be 80 feet tall! That is large enough to wreck a ship. Also, the Gulf Stream current is very strong. It could carry wreckage far away from the actual crash site. This makes it hard for rescuers to find them.

Narrator 3: But strange weather happens all over the world. And what about all of the planes that disappeared? The stormy sea wouldn't affect them.

Vincent: There are also high amounts of methane gas trapped in the ocean floor. This happens when sea plants and animals decompose. If a gas bubble reached the surface, it could sink a ship. If a gas bubble reached the air, it could explode an airplane.

Narrator 1: It still seems like there's something paranormal happening.

The Bermuda Triangle Script *(cont.)*

Vincent: I agree. There are some supernatural theories too. There are stories of huge sea monsters that sink the ships. Some people think there is a wormhole to another dimension. The planes and ships pass through the wormhole. Then they are transported to another place or world. Others believe it is aliens. The strange fireball that Columbus saw could have been a meteor. But it could also have been a spaceship. Some people think the aliens are disturbing the compasses. But all of these things are theories. No one knows anything for sure.

Narrator 2: Vincent's article created a public interest in the Bermuda Triangle. He went on to write a whole book on his theories.

Narrator 3: Over the years, more authors wrote books on the unsolved mysteries and continued to spark people's interest in the stories.

Narrator 1: The number of disappearances has lessened over time.

Narrator 2: But the mystery continues. In 1970, Pilot Bruce Gernon was flying from the Bahamas to Florida.

Narrator 3: He had flown this path many times.

Narrator 1: But on December 4, 1970, something strange happened. A thick cloud surrounded his airplane. It formed a tunnel.

Narrator 2: Pilot Gernon could see blue sky at the end of the tunnel so he headed toward it. But something took over his plane! It started moving very fast. His compass stopped working and began spinning.

Narrator 3: When Pilot Gernon escaped from the cloud tunnel, he was already above Florida. His 75-minute flight only took 45 minutes!

Narrator 1: All that is truly known about the Bermuda Triangle is that it is a place of many unsolved mysteries.

Narrator 2: Could it simply be harsh storms and strange weather?

Narrator 3: Or could it be aliens, sea monsters, or a parallel universe?

Narrator 1: What do *you* think?

The Bermuda Triangle Activity

The Bermuda Triangle

1. List two strange things that Columbus recorded when he sailed across the Sargasso Sea.

   ____

   ____

2. Why couldn't Captain Baker tell who the mystery ship belonged to?

   ____

   ____

3. How did the Bermuda Triangle get its name?

   ____

   ____

4. List three possible theories for why ships and planes disappear in the Bermuda Triangle.

   ____

   ____

   ____

Reader's Theater Reflections

Think about your performance. Color in the number of stars to show how well you did in each area.

Accuracy: I read my part correctly.	☆ ☆ ☆
Rate: I read at a pace that was not too fast or too slow.	☆ ☆ ☆
Expression: I read my character's part with feeling and emotion.	☆ ☆ ☆

List one way that you can improve your reader's theater performance.

____

____

The Bermuda Triangle Journal

There are many theories attempting to explain the Bermuda Triangle. Some are natural, and some are supernatural. But it still remains an unsolved mystery. What do you think?

____

____

____

____

____

____

____

____

____

____

____

____

____

____

____

____

____

____

The Transported Guard **Lesson Plan**

Content Objectives

- Read grade-level text orally with accuracy, appropriate rate, and expression on successive readings.
- Use knowledge of language and its conventions when writing, speaking, reading, or listening.
- Acknowledge differences in the points of view of characters, including by speaking in a different voice for each character when reading dialogue aloud.

Materials

- student copies of *The Transported Guard* Badge Art (pages 51–52)
- student copies of *The Transported Guard* Script (pages 53–58)
- student copies of *The Transported Guard* Activity (page 59)
- student copies of *The Transported Guard* Journal (page 60)
- highlighters, crayons, markers
- notecards for vocabulary game

Before Reading

1. Begin by assessing students' prior knowledge (if any) of the mystery of the teleported palace guard. Tell students that on October 24, 1593, a soldier named Gil Perez was standing guard at the Spanish Governor's palace in Manila, the capital of the Philippines. At this time in history, Spain ruled many different areas around the world. The governor had been assassinated the day before, and the guards were working longer hours to make sure the palace was safe. Gil Perez was feeling exhausted and leaned his head against the side of the building. He closed his eyes. When he opened them, he was leaning against a building in Mexico City, 9,000 miles away from Manila. Perez had no explanation for how he traveled there. He was interrogated by officials in Mexico City, who held him in prison because they did not believe his story. Two months later, a ship arrived from Manila carrying a soldier who actually knew Gil Perez and confirmed that he really was a palace guard in Manila. Perez was released and allowed to return home. Theories of teleportation, alien abduction, and wormholes are all possible ideas to explain what happened that day. It remains an unsolved mystery to this day.

2. Tell students that they will be performing a reader's theater play about the unsolved mystery of the transported guard. Distribute copies of the script. Assign students their roles based on reading proficiencies. See page 50 for a list of the reading levels for each role in *The Transported Guard* script.

The Transported Guard **Lesson Plan** *(cont.)*

Rehearsal

1. Once students have been assigned their parts, tell them to go through the entire script and highlight their parts. Then, give students time to silently read either the entire script or just their highlighted sections. Ask them to use a pencil and underline any words that they do not know or do not know how to pronounce. Go over these words together to ensure understanding.

2. This script has key vocabulary that students may not know. Consider playing a vocabulary memory game. Write the following words from the play on separate notecards: *empire, friar, teleportation, particles, abducted, expedition, assassinated, wormhole, interrogation, transcripts.* Then, write the definition of each word on separate notecards. Place all the cards facedown. Have students take turns flipping two cards over. If they match a word with the definition, they get to keep the cards. Play until all of the cards have been matched.

3. Give students time to practice their reader's theater. Remind them to speak with fluency, rate, expression, and tone. They need to play the role of the character using just their voices! Demonstrate reading a few lines in a dull, monotonous tone. Then, read the same lines with expression and ask students to explain the difference. Do the same thing with reading pace (read lines too quickly or too slowly), and then demonstrate a proper pace. Finally, whisper lines softly. Then, read them again with a proper volume. Ask students if they understand the differences.

Performance

1. There are a variety of ways for your students to perform *The Transported Guard* reader's theater. See pages 5–8 for performance ideas.

2. Distribute copies of the badges (pages 51–52). Give students time to decorate their character's badge using crayons or markers.

3. Remind students to speak loudly and clearly and with confidence! Encourage them to show emotion and feeling with their voices. Even the narrator can show emotion by reading their part with an authoritative and confident tone! If stage fright or public speaking is an issue for some students, remind them to focus on their lines instead of worrying about the audience. And finally, remind students to take deep breaths, smile, and have fun!

Assessment

1. Distribute student copies of *The Transported Guard* Activity (page 59). Go over the activity sheet together and then have students complete it independently.

2. Distribute student copies of *The Transported Guard* Journal (page 60). Remind students that what really happened to Gil Perez is still an unsolved mystery. Discuss the possible theories presented in the script, along with any of your own. Then, give students time to journal their theories.

The Transported Guard Characters

Assigning Characters

The roles in this reader's theater have been leveled to fit the individual needs of your students. When students feel confident in their reading fluency, they will engage with the character and feel comfortable performing in front of others. The goal is to have a successful performance that allows each student a chance to shine.

The Transported Guard has six roles. Each role has been designed to meet the needs of a variety of reading-level proficiencies. The characters are listed here in order of highest reading-level proficiency to lowest.

Remember that even high-level readers may struggle with giving a fluent performance. Remind students that they are performing a play using only their voices. The way they speak each word matters! Demonstrate the difference between monotone reading and reading with fluency and expression so students can understand the expectations.

You might also consider assigning nonspeaking roles to students who are reluctant to read aloud. These students could act as directors or coaches. Remind them that their role is very important. They will have to know the script extremely well and will be in charge of prompting students when it is their turn to read.

Grade 5 Reading Levels:

Narrator 1   Played by: _______________________________________

Narrator 2   Played by: _______________________________________

Friar Gaspar   Played by: _______________________________________

Grade 4/High Grade 3 Reading Levels:

Gil Perez   Played by: _______________________________________

Sailor   Played by: _______________________________________

Guard   Played by: _______________________________________

The Transported Guard Badge Art

The Transported Guard Badge Art (cont.)

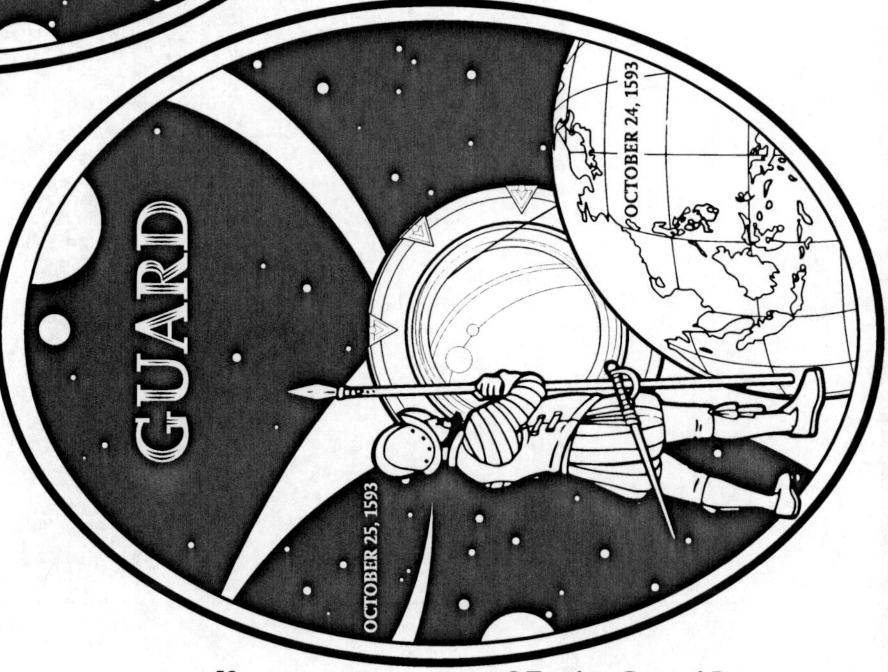

The Transported Guard Script

Characters

- Narrator 1
- Narrator 2
- Gil Perez
- Guard
- Friar Gaspar
- Sailor

Setting

Act 1 takes place on October 24, 1593, in the Philippines.
Act 2 takes place on October 25, 1593, in Mexico City.

Act 1

Narrator 1: It was October 24, 1593. Gil Perez was standing guard outside the palace. It was a typical fall day in Manila. Manila is the capital city of the Philippines.

Narrator 2: Gil Perez was a Spanish soldier. His job was to guard the Spanish governor and his palace in Manila.

Narrator 1: At that time, Spain ruled the Philippines. The Spanish Empire included many other countries. The Spanish Governor Gómez had a palace in Manila.

Gil: I am exhausted. I have been standing guard for hours. Everything is in chaos since yesterday's tragic news. We are supposed to remain here until they appoint a new governor. It could take forever. I am not sure how much longer I can stand here.

Narrator 2: The governor had died on an expedition the day before. He was assassinated by a group of pirates. Security at the palace was on high alert. The city of Manila was in a panic over the loss of Governor Gómez.

Narrator 1: The warm afternoon sun was making the guard feel sleepy.

Gil: [*yawning*] I feel like I can barely keep my eyes open. I am so drowsy. I also feel a little bit dizzy. This has been a very long day. I think I just need to close my eyes for one moment.

Narrator 2: At that moment, Soldier Perez leaned his head against the side of the palace building.

Narrator 1: What happened next may forever remain an unsolved mystery.

The Transported Guard Script *(cont.)*

Act 2

Narrator 2: Perez blinked his eyes open. He was still leaning against the side of a building.

Gil: Oh my goodness, I must have fallen asleep for a quick power nap! I do feel less exhausted. Hopefully, no one spotted me snoozing on the job. I need to get back to work. Wait a minute! Where in the world am I?

Narrator 1: Soldier Gil Perez woke up leaning against a building. The problem was, it wasn't the *same* building he fell asleep against!

Narrator 2: He looked around and realized he was very far from home. The city around him was not Manila. The citizens on the street were dressed in unfamiliar clothing. The rest of the guards were not dressed in the same uniform that Perez wore. He did not recognize a single person.

Gil: I must be dreaming. Wake up, Gil! I know what I'll do. I'll pinch my arm and if it's a dream, I won't feel it, right? OUCH! I felt that. Am I losing my mind? Or maybe this is a hallucination! That is a good explanation. I was simply overtired, and what I am seeing isn't real.

Narrator 1: Perez began walking aimlessly around the foreign city. He was talking to himself. His behavior was so strange that people began to notice him.

Gil: Can anyone tell me where I am? I am so lost, and nothing in this city looks familiar to me.

Narrator 2: A local guard approached Perez. He wanted to see if he needed some help.

Guard: Excuse me, sir? I need to ask you some questions. Your behavior is causing a scene. People are beginning to think you are unwell.

Gil: I am feeling very confused. Today is October 24th, 1593, right?

Guard: Actually, today is October 25th, 1593.

Gil: How is that even possible? Did I sleep through the night? Maybe this was all a peculiar dream. Let me ask you a question. Is the governor dead?

Guard: The governor? Which governor?

Gil: Governor Gómez of the Philippines.

The Transported Guard Script *(cont.)*

Guard: I have not heard any news of his death. When did it happen?

Gil: It happened on October 24th. I thought that was today, but I think I might have slept longer than I thought.

Guard: How did you know that Governor Gómez died yesterday?

Gil: Because I am a palace guard, and it is my job to keep the palace safe.

Guard: But why are you in Mexico City if you are supposed to be on guard in Manila? How did you get here so quickly? I watch the docks closely. No ships arrived here yesterday from the Philippines.

Gil: Mexico City?! Am I in Mexico? Ha! That is completely impossible. Even if I fell asleep on the job, there is no way I could wake up in Mexico. Is this some kind of joke?

Guard: No, this is not a joke. Your story is confusing, and I am not sure I trust you. I am going to take you in for questioning.

Narrator 1: Gil agreed to follow the guard into the office to answer questions. He was equally confused and wanted some answers of his own.

Friar Gaspar: Welcome to the Holy Office of the Inquisition of Mexico. My name is Friar Gaspar de San Agustin. I am here to record our interrogation. I keep transcripts of everything.

Gil: Interrogation? Am I in some kind of trouble?

Guard: Friar Gaspar, this man says his name is Soldier Gil Perez. He claims he is from Manila.

Friar Gaspar: Well, Soldier Perez, you are a long way from home. In fact, you are 9,000 miles away from home. What ship brought you to Mexico?

Gil: You see, that is what I am trying to figure out. I need you to believe me when I say that I was on guard in Manila on October 24th.

Friar Gaspar: So yesterday, you were working at the palace in Manila?

Gil: Yes, and I felt exhausted, so I leaned against the palace wall. I had to work a longer shift because Governor Gómez was assassinated. They were worried about the security of the palace. I closed my eyes for what felt like a brief moment. When I opened them, I was here. I understand now that I am not in Manila. But I do not have an explanation for how I got here. I would very much like to return home.

The Transported Guard Script *(cont.)*

Friar Gaspar: Governor Gómez is dead? Why are you the only person with that news? He is supposed to be on an expedition right now. I need you to tell me the truth.

Gil: This is my story, and I am sticking to it. I have no explanation for what happened to me. I am afraid and confused. I want to return home to Manila. I don't have anything else to tell you.

Friar Gaspar: Gil Perez, this sounds like witchcraft! There is no possible way for your story to be true. I am going to have you arrested until we get to the bottom of this strange matter.

Gil: Arrested? Friar Gaspar, I promise that I know nothing about magic or witchcraft. I am telling the truth. I hope you will find some way to believe me.

Narrator 1: Gil Perez spent two months in a Mexican prison. Friar Gaspar spoke with other leaders. But no one could make sense of the story.

Narrator 2: But then, something incredible happened.

Narrator 1: A boat arrived in Mexico City.

Guard: Excuse me, can you tell me where this boat sailed from?

Sailor: We sailed here from Manila. We brought supplies and items to trade.

Guard: I need a brief moment of your time, please. Will you follow me into the city? Friar Gaspar will have some questions for you.

Friar Gaspar: Welcome to the Holy Office of the Inquisition of Mexico. My name is Friar Gaspar de San Agustin. Who are you?

Sailor: My name is Diego, and I am a sailor from Manila. We were docking our ship at your port when your guard asked me to come and speak with you. What is this regarding?

Friar Gaspar: A few months ago, we had a man show up here in Mexico City. He was dressed in the official soldier attire from Manila. He had some crazy story about not remembering how he arrived here. He also told us another wild tale that Governor Gómez had been assassinated.

The Transported Guard Script *(cont.)*

Sailor: Well, surely you know that to be the truth. Governor Gómez died while on an expedition. Pirates took over his ship. It is a tragic story. It happened just a few months ago on October 24th.

Guard: Friar Gaspar, can you believe it? The story Gil Perez told us was really true.

Friar Gaspar: Hmm, well, partially true. It doesn't explain how Perez arrived in Mexico City the next day. How could he have known about the death of the governor?

Sailor: I'm sorry, sir, but did you say Gil Perez?

Friar Gaspar: Yes, he claims to have been a palace guard in Manila.

Sailor: May I see him? I think I know who he is and can help verify his story.

Narrator 1: Friar Gaspar and the guard led the sailor to the prison room.

Narrator 2: Poor Gil Perez had been puzzling over what happened to him and still had no explanation.

Sailor: Perez! It really is you! Friar Gaspar, I know this man! He used to eat his lunch by the docks in Manila. He really is a palace guard. You must let me take him back home to Manila on my ship.

Gil: Oh, my dear friend Diego! I have been waiting for this moment for months! I knew there would be a way out of here.

Guard: What do you say, Friar Gaspar? Can we release the prisoner?

Friar Gaspar: I don't know how to explain how he came here but I don't have any reason to keep him any longer. This man has confirmed his identity.

Guard: Soldier Gil Perez, you are free to return home to Manila.

Sailor: Let's rejoice, my friend! Tell me everything that happened! How in the world did you end up in Mexico City? I remember eating lunch with you on October 24th. You only had a short break that day, on account of what happened to the governor. When did you arrive in Mexico?

Gil: I arrived in Mexico on October 25th, 1593. I have no explanation for how I managed to travel 9,000 miles in one day. I have no memory of it. I am just happy to go home.

The Transported Guard Script *(cont.)*

Sailor: The city of Manila will be happy to have you home! Nobody knew what happened to you, and we all feared something tragic. I feel so lucky to bring my friend home safely! Follow me to my ship.

Friar Gaspar: Good luck to you, Gil Perez.

Narrator 1: Sailor Diego took Gil Perez safely back to the Philippines. He returned to his job as a palace guard. No strange events happened to him again.

Narrator 2: But how could his story be true? A person cannot simply close their eyes and appear in another location.

Narrator 1: There are many theories. One is teleportation. This is where particles can be instantly re-created in a new location without moving them. Scientists have been successful with teleportation on a tiny scale. So far, they can't teleport anything bigger than a particle. But the theory remains!

Narrator 2: If it wasn't teleportation, maybe there was a special energy field in the palace wall that linked to the same wall in Mexico City. So when Perez leaned against the wall, the wormhole transported him to a new location.

Narrator 1: What's a wormhole?

Narrator 2: It's kind of like a shortcut through space and time. Think of a bridge that connects two different places. If you cross it, you can end up in a new place or even in a new time period.

Narrator 1: Another possibility is aliens! Maybe he was abducted by aliens. After they were finished running tests on him, they forgot where he came from. So they erased his memory and brought him to Mexico.

Narrator 2: Whatever happened to Gil Perez that day remains an unsolved mystery.

Narrator 1: This event occurred over 400 years ago. Modern investigators doubt that it ever really happened.

Narrator 2: However, Friar Gaspar did as he promised. He wrote down transcripts of the entire conversation with Perez. Those transcripts still exist.

Narrator 1: What do *you* think happened?

The Transported Guard Activity

1. Why did Gil Perez close his eyes and lean against the palace wall?

____

____

2. Why do you think Friar Gaspar kept Perez in prison?

____

____

3. Why did Diego's story help Gil Perez get released from prison?

____

____

4. Do you think this mystery will ever be solved? Why or why not?

____

____

____

Reader's Theater Reflections

Think about your performance. Color in the number of stars to show how well you did in each area.

Accuracy: I read my part correctly.	☆ ☆ ☆
Rate: I read at a pace that was not too fast or too slow.	☆ ☆ ☆
Expression: I read my character's part with feeling and emotion.	☆ ☆ ☆

List one way that you can improve your reader's theater performance.

____

____

The Transported Guard Journal

Nobody knows how Gil Perez traveled from Manila to Mexico City in less than one day. It remains an unsolved mystery. What do you think happened?

The Transported Guard

Unidentified Flying Objects Lesson Plan

Content Objectives

- Read grade-level text orally with accuracy, appropriate rate, and expression on successive readings.
- Use knowledge of language and its conventions when writing, speaking, reading, or listening.
- Acknowledge differences in the points of view of characters, including by speaking in a different voice for each character when reading dialogue aloud.

Materials

- student copies of *Unidentified Flying Objects* Badge Art (pages 64–65)
- student copies of *Unidentified Flying Objects* Script (pages 66–71)
- student copies of *Unidentified Flying Objects* Activity (page 72)
- student copies of *Unidentified Flying Objects* Journal (page 73)
- highlighters, crayons, markers

Before Reading

1. Begin by assessing students' prior knowledge (if any) of the mystery of unidentified flying objects, or UFOs. In the early 1900s, the world was still learning about flight and planes were finally taking off successfully. But in the mid 1900s, a few people started seeing aircraft that looked nothing like typical airplanes and jets. Tell students that they will read a script about three different encounters with UFOs and how the world is still uncertain as to what these aircraft are and if they really do come from outer space. The first eyewitness encounter was by pilot Kenneth Arnold, whose report is full of detail and factual evidence, making him a reliable witness. The second encounter is what is known today as the Roswell Incident, where an unidentifiable object crashed into a farm field in New Mexico and the government gave a confusing story about what really happened that day. The third event happened a few years later when two Air Force pilots were sent out to chase a UFO and then vanished from radar. They were never seen again. The general public complained for years that the U.S. government was hiding its knowledge of aliens and UFOs. But today, the government confirms that about 6 percent of UFO sightings truly cannot be explained, even by the air force.

2. Tell students that they will be performing a reader's theater play about the unsolved mystery of what UFOs are and where they come from. Distribute copies of the script. Assign students their roles based on reading proficiencies. See page 63 for a list of the reading levels for each role in the *Unidentified Flying Objects* script.

Unidentified Flying Objects
Lesson Plan *(cont.)*

Rehearsal

1. Once students have been assigned their parts, tell them to go through the entire script and highlight their parts. Then, give students time to silently read either the entire script or just their highlighted sections. Ask them to use a pencil and underline any words that they do not know or do not know how to pronounce. Go over these words together to ensure understanding.

2. This script has key vocabulary that students may not know. Consider creating a word wall. Write the following words from the play on the board or a piece of chart paper: *wreckage, fiber optic, weather balloon, atomic bomb, vertigo, portal, mirage, debris, hieroglyphics, radar.* Ask students to help you define each one. Write the definitions next to the words. If students are unsure of the definitions, have them read the dictionary definitions to you.

3. Give students time to practice their reader's theater. Remind them to speak with fluency, rate, expression, and tone. They need to play the role of the character using just their voices! Demonstrate reading a few lines in a dull, monotonous tone. Then, read the same lines with expression and ask students to explain the difference. Do the same thing with reading pace (read lines too quickly or too slowly), and then demonstrate a proper pace. Finally, whisper lines softly. Then, read them again with a proper volume. Ask students if they understand the differences.

Performance

1. There are a variety of ways for your students to perform the *Unidentified Flying Objects* reader's theater. See pages 5–8 for performance ideas.

2. Distribute copies of the badges (pages 64–65). Give students time to decorate their character's badge using crayons or markers.

3. Remind students to speak loudly and clearly and with confidence! Encourage them to show emotion and feeling with their voices. Even the narrator can show emotion by reading their part with an authoritative and confident tone! If stage fright or public speaking is an issue for some students, remind them to focus on their lines instead of worrying about the audience. And finally, remind students to take deep breaths, smile, and have fun!

Assessment

1. Distribute student copies of the *Unidentified Flying Objects* Activity (page 72). Go over the activity sheet together and then have students complete it independently.

2. Distribute student copies of the *Unidentified Flying Objects* Journal (page 73). Remind students that while we know UFOs exist, we still have no explanation for what they are or where they come from. It is still an unsolved mystery. Discuss the possible theories presented in the script, along with any of your own. Then, give students time to journal their theories.

Unidentified Flying Objects **Characters**

Assigning Characters

The roles in this reader's theater have been leveled to fit the individual needs of your students. When students feel confident in their reading fluency, they will engage with the character and feel comfortable performing in front of others. The goal is to have a successful performance that allows each student a chance to shine.

Unidentified Flying Objects has six roles. Each role has been designed to meet the needs of a variety of reading-level proficiencies. The characters are listed here in order of highest reading-level proficiency to lowest.

Remember that even high-level readers may struggle with giving a fluent performance. Remind students that they are performing a play using only their voices. The way they speak each word matters! Demonstrate the difference between monotone reading and reading with fluency and expression so students can understand the expectations.

You might also consider assigning nonspeaking roles to students who are reluctant to read aloud. These students could act as directors or coaches. Remind them that their role is very important. They will have to know the script extremely well and will be in charge of prompting students when it is their turn to read.

Grade 5 Reading Levels:

Narrator 1   Played by: _______________________________

Narrator 2   Played by: _______________________________

Pilot Kenneth Arnold   Played by: _______________________________

Grade 4/High Grade 3 Reading Levels:

First Lieutenant Felix Moncla   Played by: _______________________________

Major Jesse Marcel   Played by: _______________________________

Rancher William Brazel   Played by: _______________________________

Unidentified Flying Objects Badge Art

Unidentified Flying Objects Badge Art (cont.)

Unidentified Flying Objects Script

Characters
- Narrator 1
- Narrator 2
- Pilot Kenneth Arnold
- Rancher William Brazel
- Major Jesse Marcel
- First Lieutenant Felix Moncla

Setting

Act 1 takes place on June 24, 1947, in an airplane flying over Washington State. Act 2 takes place in New Mexico less than a month later. Act 3 takes place in 1953 in an Air Force jet.

Act 1

Narrator 1: On June 24, 1947, Pilot Kenneth Arnold was flying above Mount Rainier. He was looking for the wreckage of a plane that had gone missing.

Narrator 2: After searching for a while, he decided to return to the airport. But something flashed outside his airplane window.

Kenneth: What was that bright flashing light? I hope it wasn't another airplane. I'll be extra cautious just in case.

Narrator 1: The flashing light turned out to be nine separate shiny objects.

Kenneth: I have never seen anything like this! It must be a new kind of military jet. These aircraft are shaped like giant teacup saucers. I estimate that they are around 45 feet across. They are all flying together in a chain that looks like a V-formation. I wonder if this is a test-pilot group.

Narrator 2: Pilot Arnold continued to watch the aircraft flying above the mountains.

Kenneth: The snowy background of Mount Rainier is giving me the best view of these strange new planes. The way they can fly is truly astounding! They are circular, but they don't seem to spin. They move the way skipping stones do across the surface of water. They weave in and out of the mountains like the tail of a kite. When they flip sideways, they look so thin and flat. It's almost like they are little pie pans flying through the sky! I am going to open my plane's side window so I can get a clear view.

Narrator 1: Arnold wanted to observe as much as he could about this new aircraft.

Unidentified Flying Objects Script *(cont.)*

Kenneth: They are flying at speeds that appear faster than any aircraft I have ever seen. I want to see if I can track their speed. I am going to clock them using my instrument panel. Let's see how fast they travel from Mount Rainier to Mount Adams. One minute; one minute, thirty seconds; one minute, forty-five seconds! Wow, that seems incredibly fast. I know the distance between those mountains is 50 miles. According to my calculations, they are flying 1,700 miles per hour!

Narrator 2: Arnold watched the nine flying saucers soar out of sight. He landed his own plane and was excited to tell people about what he saw.

Narrator 1: There was only one problem. The U.S. Army said they knew nothing about the flying saucers that he saw.

Kenneth: Initially, I was certain they were new military planes. But the government denied that they have any aircraft like the ones I saw. There were no test flights above those mountains that day. My only conclusion is that what I saw was *not* from this world. A few other pilots have told me similar stories of seeing these flying discs. That helped me feel confident that what I saw was not a mirage.

Act 2

Narrator 2: Less than one month later, another strange event happened.

Narrator 1: Rancher William Brazel woke up early to start his work day.

William: [*yawns*] Boy, I had a hard time sleeping through that thunderstorm last night. The sky was lit up like the Fourth of July! I have never seen so many flashes of lightning. The booming thunder kept all of the animals awake too. What an exhausting night!

Narrator 2: Despite the stormy night, the morning seemed typical. Nothing seemed unusual until William went out to the sheep pasture.

William: I'm glad I started my day early. The storm is over, and it's going to be a hot summer day here in New Mexico. Hmmm . . . that's strange. I wonder why all the sheep are huddled in the corner. They look spooked. I guess the storm kept them up all night too.

Narrator 1: William began to walk around the pasture. The field was covered in strange materials.

Unidentified Flying Objects Script *(cont.)*

William: What on earth is all of this junk? Something must have crashed into the field last night. It looks like big strips of tinfoil and rubber. Some of it is paper thin and really shiny. There are cardboard pieces and sticks too. Where did all this debris come from? It looks like it fell straight out of the sky. What a mystery! I am going to take some of the wreckage home with me to show my wife and kids. Maybe they will have an explanation.

Narrator 2: William took a box full of the debris home to his family. They had no idea what it was.

Narrator 1: He didn't think much about it until a few weeks later. That is when he heard reports about Kenneth Arnold and the mysterious flying saucers.

William: Oh my goodness! What if one of those flying saucers crashed into the field? I think I better report my findings to the police. I still have a box of the unusual material to show them.

Narrator 2: William reported his findings to the local sheriff. The sheriff contacted Major Jesse Marcel, who worked at the Roswell Army Air Field.

Narrator 1: William met with Jesse and showed him around the field.

Jesse: Thank you for taking me to the crash site, Mr. Brazel. I am not sure I will have the answers you are looking for, but I will do my best.

William: Thank you, Major Marcel. At first, I thought it must be some kind of a kite. But the more I looked at it, the more I realized that this wasn't a kite. In addition, there are a variety of materials that look like sticks and rubber and cardboard, but I couldn't bend them or even burn them. I was a little embarrassed to claim it could be one of those flying saucers that the newspapers are buzzing about. But I have never seen anything like this before.

Jesse: I am sure there is a logical explanation for this. Let's take a look.

Narrator 2: Jesse walked around the field and collected more of the materials in a box.

Narrator 1: One piece, in particular, caught his attention.

Jesse: Look at this piece! It is a beam with strange lettering that almost looks like hieroglyphics. I have never seen this language before. This wreckage is definitely not pieces of a kite. Thank you, Mr. Brazel. I will take this debris back to Roswell.

Unidentified Flying Objects Script *(cont.)*

Narrator 2: But on the drive, Major Jesse Marcel made a quick decision. He stopped at his home. It was 2:00 in the morning.

Jesse: Children, wake up! I want to show you this box before I turn it in. I have a feeling it will be classified, and you might never have a chance to see it again. This box is full of wreckage found in a field nearby. I am certain this material is not from our world. Look at this strange lettering. I believe it came from outer space. It could be linked to those flying discs that the pilots keep seeing.

Narrator 1: The kids looked through the material in the box. They were amazed at the way the material felt. The thin pieces of foil were impossible to tear, break, or burn. When they crumpled it, it would return to its original state. There were silky strands of string that could transfer light, similar to a fiber-optic cable.

Narrator 2: Major Marcel sent his kids back to bed and returned to Roswell. He told the military what he discovered. The newspapers ran a story the next day that read, "The Roswell Army Air Field has captured a flying disc on a ranch in the Roswell region!"

Jesse: This is where it begins to get complicated. I told everyone the truth. I thought they believed me. But then the air force ran a new story that said we made a mistake. The debris was not from a flying saucer but instead from a weather balloon. They made me pose for newspaper photos holding a broken weather balloon. I was told to keep quiet and not tell any more people anything about the incident.

William: The government contacted me too. I was told that what I found that day was a weather balloon. I was to remain quiet about the incident. I was embarrassed when they ran that second story because I had already told my family and neighbors that I was certain it was a flying saucer.

Narrator 1: Major Marcel and William Brazel were told that it was necessary to change the story for security reasons. They both felt forced to go along with it.

Narrator 2: Later, the air force explained why they made up the weather balloon story. It was not to cover up aliens. It was to cover up a top-secret project called Project Mogul. The army was putting microphones on small weather balloons. These balloons were trying to detect sound waves from countries running atomic bomb tests.

Unidentified Flying Objects Script *(cont.)*

Jesse: Baloney! I saw the wreckage with my own eyes. The material was nothing made on this Earth. I think they are hiding the fact that they found things that they don't know how to explain. Unidentifiable things! I continued to research the mysterious crash. People started calling it the Roswell Incident. The story grew to include tales of tiny alien bodies being found at the crash site. At this point, anything is possible.

Act 3

Narrator 1: Public interest in the unidentified flying objects (or UFOs) grew. People were either excited or terrified to believe that there was life beyond planet Earth.

Narrator 2: Things began to calm down for a few years. But then in 1953, another incident happened.

Narrator 1: On November 23, 1953, First Lieutenant Felix Moncla received a call for a special mission.

Felix: Hello, this is Lieutenant Moncla. Yes, I am available to help out the U.S. Air Defense Command. What do you need? You say there is an unidentifiable aircraft flying over Lake Superior? But that is restricted air space. I will pilot the jet, and Second Lieutenant Robert Wilson can watch the radar. We're on it!

Narrator 2: Lieutenant Moncla and Lieutenant Wilson took off from Kinross Air Force Base in Michigan.

Felix: Hello, ground control. We see the unknown object on our radar, but we are having trouble chasing it. It seems to keep changing course. It is flying in strange patterns. Lieutenant Wilson keeps losing it on the radar. But no worries! I am flying an F-89C Scorpion jet. I will catch it in no time.

Narrator 1: Ground control was watching both blips on the radar closely. One was the unidentified aircraft. The other was Felix's jet.

Narrator 2: The blips on the screen were headed right for each other.

Felix: We are in pursuit! I feel like this is a game of cat chasing mouse. Whoever is flying this craft has extreme skills. I have tracked them from 25,000 feet down to just 7,000. We are now about 70 miles from the southern shore of Lake Superior. We have been chasing them for 160 miles now. But something seems strange. I have never seen an aircraft fly this way before. I have tried to make radio contact, but there is no response. Maybe it's a Canadian jet.

Unidentified Flying Objects Script *(cont.)*

Narrator 1: But there were no Canadian aircraft in that air space at that time.

Felix: Lieutenant Wilson and I keep joking that maybe we are in pursuit of one of those UFOs! He is still having trouble tracking the strange craft on radar but we are getting closer. I think we are right behind it.

Narrator 1: Ground control watched as the two blips on the screen merged into one. It looked as though they locked together and became one.

Narrator 2: Did they crash into each other? What happened?

Narrator 1: To everyone's amazement, the unidentified aircraft emerged on radar. It veered off course and then vanished.

Narrator 2: Lieutenant Moncla and Lieutenant Wilson's jet disappeared from radar. It looked as though they were swallowed up by the other aircraft.

Narrator 1: The U.S. military sent out search and rescue teams. But there was no trace of Felix, Robert, or their jet.

Narrator 2: The case was closed when the military declared that Felix suffered from vertigo. This is a condition that causes dizziness. They said he crashed the jet into the lake.

Narrator 1: But when investigators tried to reopen the case, the file was missing from official air force reports.

Narrator 2: UFO researchers believe that the jet was taken aboard the UFO ship. Or, Moncla flew into an alien portal to outer space!

Narrator 1: In 2021, the U.S. government confirmed that UFOs exist. That just means that there are videos and photographs of actual unidentifiable flying objects. Nobody knows where these UFOs are from or if they have alien pilots.

Narrator 2: The mystery of UFOs and life beyond our planet continues to be an unsolved mystery. What do *you* think?

Unidentified Flying Objects

Unidentified Flying Objects Activity

1. Name two things that Kenneth Arnold thought were unusual about the UFOs he saw.

____

____

2. Do you believe that the wreckage found by Rancher William Brazel and Major Jesse Marcel was really from outer space?

____

____

3. What do you think happened to Felix Moncla and Robert Wilson?

____

____

4. Do you think this mystery will ever be solved? Why or why not?

____

____

____

Reader's Theater Reflections

Think about your performance. Color in the number of stars to show how well you did in each area.

Accuracy: I read my part correctly.	☆ ☆ ☆
Rate: I read at a pace that was not too fast or too slow.	☆ ☆ ☆
Expression: I read my character's part with feeling and emotion.	☆ ☆ ☆

List one way that you can improve your reader's theater performance.

____

____

Unidentified Flying Objects Journal

Reports of UFO sightings have continued since the mid 1900s. Where these aircraft come from and who the pilots are remains an unsolved mystery. What do you think?

The Man from Taured Lesson Plan

Content Objectives

- Read grade-level text orally with accuracy, appropriate rate, and expression on successive readings.
- Use knowledge of language and its conventions when writing, speaking, reading, or listening.
- Acknowledge differences in the points of view of characters, including by speaking in a different voice for each character when reading dialogue aloud.

Materials

- student copies of *The Man from Taured* Badge Art (pages 77–78)
- student copies of *The Man from Taured* Script (pages 79–84)
- student copies of *The Man from Taured* Activity (page 85)
- student copies of *The Man from Taured* Journal (page 86)
- highlighters, crayons, markers

Before Reading

1. Begin by assessing students' prior knowledge (if any) of the legend of the traveler from Taured. Some people think it is just a hoax or an urban legend. Others think there is more to the story and that there were enough witnesses to consider it to be truth. In 1954, a man arrived at the Haneda Airport in Tokyo, Japan. He had to go through customs and show his passport. He told the agents that he was traveling from his home country of Taured. They had never heard of Taured and were shocked when he displayed an authentic-looking passport that was issued in Taured. When they asked him to point out his country on a map, he showed them the small country between Spain and France that was known as Andorra. But he insisted that he had never heard of Andorra before and that country was called Taured. His favorite hotel in Tokyo had no record of him ever being a guest there. The agents arranged for him to stay the night in a hotel while they sorted the situation out. The hotel room had no exit except for the door, and there was a guard out front of his door all night. But the next morning he was gone without a trace! There are theories of time travel, multiverses, parallel universes, and more! But it still remains an unsolved mystery.

2. Tell students that they will be performing a reader's theater play about the unsolved mystery of the man from Taured. Distribute copies of the script. Assign students their roles based on reading proficiencies. See page 76 for a list of the reading levels for each role in *The Man from Taured* script.

The Man from Taured **Lesson Plan** *(cont.)*

Rehearsal

1. Once students have been assigned their parts, tell them to go through the entire script and highlight their parts. Then, give students time to silently read either the entire script or just their highlighted sections. Ask them to use a pencil and underline any words that they do not know or do not know how to pronounce. Go over these words together to ensure understanding.

2. This script has key vocabulary that students may not know. Have students write down the following words from the play on a piece of paper: *passport, customs, hoax, parallel universe, origin, colleague, turbulence, multiverses, wormholes, predicament.* Have students look up the definition of each and either write the definition in their own words, or draw a picture to match each word.

3. Give students time to practice their reader's theater. Remind them to speak with fluency, rate, expression, and tone. They need to play the role of the character using just their voices! Demonstrate reading a few lines in a dull, monotonous tone. Then, read the same lines with expression and ask students to explain the difference. Do the same thing with reading pace (read lines too quickly or too slowly), and then demonstrate a proper pace. Finally, whisper lines softly. Then, read them again with a proper volume. Ask students if they understand the differences.

Performance

1. There are a variety of ways for your students to perform *The Man from Taured* reader's theater. See pages 5–8 for performance ideas.

2. Distribute copies of the badges (pages 77–78). Give students time to decorate their character's badge using crayons or markers.

3. Remind students to speak loudly and clearly and with confidence! Encourage them to show emotion and feeling with their voices. Even the narrator can show emotion by reading their part with an authoritative and confident tone! If stage fright or public speaking is an issue for some students, remind them to focus on their lines instead of worrying about the audience. And finally, remind students to take deep breaths, smile, and have fun!

Assessment

1. Distribute student copies of *The Man from Taured* Activity (page 85). Go over the activity sheet together, and then have students complete it independently.

2. Distribute student copies of *The Man from Taured* Journal (page 86). Remind students that the traveler from Taured is still an unsolved mystery. Discuss the possible theories presented in the script, along with any of your own. Then, give students time to journal their theories.

The Man from Taured Characters

Assigning Characters

The roles in this reader's theater have been leveled to fit the individual needs of your students. When students feel confident in their reading fluency, they will engage with the character and feel comfortable performing in front of others. The goal is to have a successful performance that allows each student a chance to shine.

The Man from Taured has six roles. Each role has been designed to meet the needs of a variety of reading-level proficiencies. The characters are listed here in order of highest reading-level proficiency to lowest.

Remember that even high-level readers may struggle with giving a fluent performance. Remind students that they are performing a play using only their voices. The way they speak each word matters! Demonstrate the difference between monotone reading and reading with fluency and expression so students can understand the expectations.

You might also consider assigning nonspeaking roles to students who are reluctant to read aloud. These students could act as directors or coaches. Remind them that their role is very important. They will have to know the script extremely well and will be in charge of prompting students when it is their turn to read.

Grade 5 Reading Levels:

Narrator 1 Played by: _______________________________

Narrator 2 Played by: _______________________________

Guard Suzuki Played by: _______________________________

Grade 4/High Grade 3 Reading Levels:

Traveler from Taured Played by: _______________________________

Customs Agent Sato Played by: _______________________________

Customs Agent Tachi Played by: _______________________________

The Man from Taured Badge Art

The Man from Taured Badge Art (cont.)

 78

The Man from Taured Script

Characters
- Narrator 1
- Narrator 2
- Customs Agent Sato
- Traveler from Taured
- Customs Agent Tachi
- Guard Suzuki

Setting

Act 1 takes place in 1954 at the Haneda Airport in Tokyo, Japan. Act 2 takes place the next day in a hotel in Tokyo.

Act 1

Narrator 1: In July 1954, a plane arrives at Haneda Airport, located in Tokyo, Japan. The following events will remain an unsolved mystery to this day and possibly forever.

Narrator 2: The passengers aboard the flight exit the plane and head into the airport. They all make their way to the customs department. All international passengers have to go through customs.

Narrator 1: Customs is a security checkpoint at an airport. International passengers must show their passports. A passport is a travel document that proves a passenger's country of origin.

Narrator 2: On this day, a European businessman waits in the customs line for his turn. He is dressed in an expensive-looking suit and is holding his briefcase and his passport.

Sato: Next passenger in line, please step forward. Good afternoon, sir. Why are you visiting Japan today?

Traveler: For a routine business trip. In fact, this is the third time I have been to Japan for business this year. Tokyo in July has some intense summer heat.

Sato: Yes, we are experiencing a fairly hot summer month. How long is your business trip intended to last here in Tokyo?

Traveler: I only intend to stay in Tokyo for the week. I am staying at my favorite hotel down the street called the Royal Park Hotel. They have the most comfortable beds! I sleep better there than I do in my own bed at home.

Sato: I trust your stay will be a pleasant one. Lastly, I just need to confirm which country you are traveling here from.

Traveler: I am from Taured.

The Man from Taured Script *(cont.)*

Sato: Excuse me? I didn't hear your response correctly. What is your country of origin?

Traveler: Taured.

Sato: I need you to spell it out for me.

Traveler: T-A-U-R-E-D. Taured is the small country located between France and Spain.

Sato: May I please see your passport?

Traveler: Certainly.

Narrator 1: Customs agent Sato scanned the traveler's passport. The machine beeped and displayed an error message. Sato flipped through the passport. The man had traveled frequently. There was evidence of his previous trips to Japan. And sure enough, the first page of the passport clearly stated that it was issued in the country of Taured.

Sato: There seems to be a slight problem. I have worked here for years, and I have never encountered someone from Taured. Please wait here while I speak with my colleague, Agent Tachi.

Narrator 2: Customs Agent Sato took the passport to his coworker, Agent Tachi.

Sato: Tachi, I need your assistance! I am slightly embarrassed. I have a traveler here from Taured, and when I tried scanning his passport, it gave me an error message.

Tachi: Where in the world is Taured? That must be his town or neighborhood. What country is he traveling from?

Sato: I was not aware that the country of Taured existed either. But look at his passport. It truly is from the country of Taured.

Tachi: This passport looks authentic, but it is impossible. There is no official country of Taured. Maybe he is a foreign spy or something. I will interrogate him, and we will figure this mystery out.

Narrator 1: Agent Sato and Agent Tachi returned to the mysterious traveler from Taured. He looked tired and exasperated.

Traveler: Am I in some sort of trouble? You can search my briefcase if you would like, but I don't have anything that's not permitted. I have had an exceedingly long day and just want to check into my favorite hotel.

The Man from Taured Script *(cont.)*

Tachi: Hello, sir. My name is Agent Tachi, and I need to ask you a few more questions. Please follow us to the Special Examination Room.

Narrator 2: The traveler followed the two agents into a small office. He took a seat at a table and sighed.

Tachi: Your passport states that you are from the country of Taured. Is this the only passport you own?

Traveler: Yes, of course that is my only passport. I was born in Taured and have never lived anywhere else. I often travel for business, but Taured is my home.

Tachi: Is French your native language?

Traveler: Yes, you can probably hear my accent. Tauredians speak French. But surely you already know that?

Sato: But you speak Japanese perfectly.

Traveler: I speak many languages. Like I already said, I frequently travel for business, so it is important that I can communicate with people.

Tachi: Now, I am going to display a world map for you to examine. Can you please point to the country of Taured?

Narrator 1: The customs agent displayed a large world map. The traveler instantly pointed to a small country located on the border of France and Spain.

Traveler: Right here is my homeland of Taured in Europe. People often mistake us for Spain or France, but no, we are an independent country.

Tachi: Sir, that is the country of Andorra. Are you from Andorra?

Traveler: Andorra? I have never heard of that. I told you I am from Taured, and I provided my passport and even showed you Taured on the map. I am confused as to why I am still being questioned.

Sato: Sir, look closely at the map, and pay attention to the labels. You pointed to the country of Andorra. There is no Taured, and in fact, there has never been a country of Taured.

Tachi: Sir, you arrived on the plane from Manila, correct?

Traveler: Yes, in the Philippines. That's still a country, right?

The Man from Taured Script *(cont.)*

Tachi: Yes, the Philippines is a country. How did you get to the Philippines?

Traveler: I departed on a plane from Taured. You can verify that flight on my passport. It was stamped when I entered the Philippines.

Narrator 2: Agents Tachi and Sato checked the passport and confirmed that he traveled from Taured to the Philippines before arriving in Japan.

Tachi: This must be a prank or some kind of hoax. Taured does not exist, and I cannot let you go with a counterfeit passport.

Traveler: My country exists! I do not know why you want to call it Andorra, but it exists. It is getting late, and I want to check into my hotel.

Sato: You said you were staying at the Royal Park Hotel, correct?

Traveler: Yes, it is where I always stay when I am in Tokyo.

Narrator 1: Agent Sato called the Royal Park Hotel to confirm the traveler's confirmation. They had no record of him ever staying at their hotel.

Sato: Sir, are you telling us the truth? The Royal Park Hotel has no record of you staying there.

Traveler: But that can't possibly be true because even the hotel manager knows me! I stayed at the Royal Park Hotel a few months ago on my last business trip. I made reservations for the whole week. This must be a joke, or maybe it's a nightmare.

Tachi: I have arranged for you to spend the night in the airport hotel next door. Suzuki, our guard, will escort you there. You aren't in any trouble, but I cannot let you go until I have security clearance. We will try to sort this out in the morning.

Narrator 2: The weary traveler sighed and gathered up his things and followed the guard out of the airport.

Suzuki: My name is Suzuki, and I will be escorting you to your hotel room for the night. Do you mind if we walk there? I love the breezy summer nights here in Tokyo. It's a welcome change to standing guard in the airport all night.

Traveler: Walking is fine.

Suzuki: The customs agents provided me with special instructions to spend my whole shift outside your room. Do you plan on trying to escape?

The Man from Taured Script *(cont.)*

Traveler: Escape? No. I just don't understand anything that is happening right now. I am not a criminal. I have never even had a speeding ticket. I am just here on a business trip.

Suzuki: I am an excellent judge of character and I believe you. They said you traveled here from Andorra. I visited your beautiful country once many years ago.

Traveler: I am NOT from Andorra and have never even heard of that country. I am from Taured. I have no clue how to explain why your maps are labeled incorrectly.

Suzuki: That is very peculiar. Let's talk about Taured. What specific details can you tell me about the country?

Traveler: It is surrounded by mountains, and we often get snow. It's why I am not used to the hot summer temperatures here in Tokyo. I am actually from Les Escaldes.

Suzuki: I have been to Les Escaldes! That is the charming village with the natural hot springs.

Traveler: YES! So I am not losing my mind! Our capital city is Taured la Vella.

Suzuki: Well, no, here it is called Andorra la Vella. But let me ponder this for a moment. I have a theory. Did you notice anything strange on the plane ride here?

Traveler: The plane was stormy, and there was a lot of turbulence. I slept most of the flight. However, the seat next to me was empty for the first half of the flight, but when I woke up, there was a new passenger next to me. I found that peculiar.

Suzuki: You don't even have to say anything else. I have solved the mystery! You traveled here from a parallel universe! Something must have happened on that plane and you entered our universe by mistake.

Traveler: Now I am beginning to think everyone here is wacky.

Suzuki: Initially, I thought you might be a time traveler. I read a lot of science fiction stories, but you don't look like you are from the future.

Traveler: That's because I am not. I am from 1954, just like you are.

Suzuki: Exactly! But some people think there are countless universes just like ours that are existing somehow at the same time. You must have just passed through a link between the two.

Traveler: I did not pass through anything. I simply flew on an airplane.

The Man from Taured Script *(cont.)*

Suzuki: I believe there are wormholes that link the multiverses, almost like hidden doorways. That also explains the new passenger next to you on the flight. I bet all of the other passengers on the flight after you woke up were new. Your universe sounds very similar to ours, which is why you didn't think you were in a strange world when you arrived here. Plus, it explains why you know about the Royal Park Hotel, but they don't know you. You have stayed at that hotel in your universe, just not in ours. Well, here is your hotel room. Do you need anything?

Traveler: No, I just need to sleep and forget about this dreadful day. But thank you, Mr. Suzuki. I don't believe a word you said, but you are the only person who seems to believe me.

Suzuki: I will be outside if you need anything. I will continue to analyze the multiverse theory. It's the best explanation to describe your predicament. I'm going to think about how we can get you back to the right realm!

Act 2

Narrator 2: Agents Tachi and Sato met with Suzuki in the morning. They knocked on the hotel room door. There was no answer.

Narrator 1: Suzuki unlocked the door and gasped. The room was completely empty. The man from Taured and all his belongings were gone.

Sato: Suzuki! Did you let him escape?

Suzuki: No, he went to sleep and never came out.

Tachi: This hotel room is on the thirteenth floor. There is no way he could have gotten out.

Suzuki: He must have found a way to return to his universe! Well done, traveler from Taured!

Narrator 2: Nobody ever figured out what happened to the traveler from Taured. Was he really from a parallel universe?

Narrator 1: Or was the entire story a hoax? There is no remaining evidence to prove this story ever happened. It could just be an urban legend.

Narrator 2: What do *you* think?

The Man from Taured Activity

1. Why was the man from Taured visiting Japan?

____

____

2. What happened when he showed the agents where Taured was on the map?

____

____

3. What was Suzuki's theory about what happened to the traveler?

____

____

4. Do you think this mystery will ever be solved? Do you think it is even a real story? Why or why not?

____

____

____

Reader's Theater Reflections

Think about your performance. Color in the number of stars to show how well you did in each area.

Accuracy: I read my part correctly.	☆ ☆ ☆
Rate: I read at a pace that was not too fast or too slow.	☆ ☆ ☆
Expression: I read my character's part with feeling and emotion.	☆ ☆ ☆

List one way that you can improve your reader's theater performance.

____

The Man from Taured Journal

The account of the man from Taured could be real, or it could just be an urban legend. It still remains an unsolved mystery. What do you think?

____

____

____

____

____

____

____

____

____

____

____

____

____

____

____

____

____

____

____

____

The Lost City Lesson Plan

Content Objectives

- Read grade-level text orally with accuracy, appropriate rate, and expression on successive readings.
- Use knowledge of language and its conventions when writing, speaking, reading, or listening.
- Acknowledge differences in the points of view of characters, including by speaking in a different voice for each character when reading dialogue aloud.

Materials

- student copies of *The Lost City* Badge Art (pages 90–91)
- student copies of *The Lost City* Script (pages 92–97)
- student copies of *The Lost City* Activity (page 98)
- student copies of *The Lost City* Journal (page 99)
- highlighters, crayons, markers

Before Reading

1. Begin by assessing students' prior knowledge (if any) of the lost city of Atlantis. Provide the following background knowledge: A Greek philosopher named Plato lived in the years of 428 BCE to 328 BCE. He is known for writing down dialogues of conversations he had with other philosophers in the form of stories. One story is titled "Timaeus and Critias." It tells a tale about a legendary utopian city called Atlantis. It was located on an island that was lush and full of exotic produce and animals. The climate was mild. The people had everything they could possibly wish for. One day, Poseidon, god of the sea, married a mortal woman living on the island. Together they had five sets of twin boys. The oldest son was named Atlas. They named him the first king, and the other brothers ruled over the adjoining nine regions of the city. The center of the city held a temple devoted to Poseidon. The city of Atlantis flourished. The people were educated, skilled, and had advanced technology. They built bridges, buildings, and irrigation systems. They also built ships and had a skilled army. But over time, the people became greedy and conquered neighboring lands. They stopped worshipping the gods, who in return, became angry. One day, the Atlanteans waged war on the nearby city of Athens and lost. Poseidon and the other gods punished the city of Atlantis by plaguing them with earthquakes and storms. In one day, the island sunk to the bottom of the ocean. Today, historians disagree on the meaning of Plato's tale. Was it just to teach a lesson to the people? Or did the actual city of Atlantis really exist? If it did, will we ever find it?

2. Tell students that they will be performing a reader's theater play about the unsolved mystery of the lost city of Atlantis. Distribute copies of the script. Assign students their roles based on reading proficiencies. See page 89 for a list of the reading levels for each role in *The Lost City* script.

The Lost City Lesson Plan *(cont.)*

Rehearsal

1. Once students have been assigned their parts, tell them to go through the entire script and highlight their parts. Then, give students time to silently read either the entire script or just their highlighted sections. Ask them to use a pencil and underline any words that they do not know or do not know how to pronounce. Go over these words together to ensure understanding.

2. This script has key vocabulary that students may not know. Have students write down the following words from the play on a piece of paper: *philosopher, moral, utopian, documentary, politician, zooplankton, mortal, irrigation, shoal, expertise, oxidized*. Have students look up the definition of each word and then quiz one another on their definitions.

3. Give students time to practice their reader's theater. Remind them to speak with fluency, rate, expression, and tone. They need to play the role of the character using just their voices! Demonstrate reading a few lines in a dull, monotonous tone. Then, read the same lines with expression and ask students to explain the difference. Do the same thing with reading pace (read lines too quickly or too slowly), and then demonstrate a proper pace. Finally, whisper lines softly. Then, read them again with a proper volume. Ask students if they understand the differences.

Performance

1. There are a variety of ways for your students to perform *The Lost City* reader's theater. See pages 5–8 for performance ideas.

2. Distribute copies of the badges (pages 90–91). Give students time to decorate their character's badge using crayons or markers.

3. Remind students to speak loudly and clearly and with confidence! Encourage them to show emotion and feeling with their voices. Even the narrator can show emotion by reading their part with an authoritative and confident tone! If stage fright or public speaking is an issue for some students, remind them to focus on their lines instead of worrying about the audience. And finally, remind students to take deep breaths, smile, and have fun!

Assessment

1. Distribute student copies of *The Lost City* Activity (page 98). Go over the activity sheet together, and then have students complete it independently.

2. Distribute student copies of *The Lost City* Journal (page 99). Remind students that despite many claims to have found it, the city of Atlantis remains lost. It is still an unsolved mystery. Discuss the possible theories presented in the script, along with any of your own. Then, give students time to journal their theories.

The Lost City Characters

Assigning Characters

The roles in this reader's theater have been leveled to fit the individual needs of your students. When students feel confident in their reading fluency, they will engage with the character and feel comfortable performing in front of others. The goal is to have a successful performance that allows each student a chance to shine.

The Lost City has six roles. Each role has been designed to meet the needs of a variety of reading-level proficiencies. The characters are listed here in order of highest reading-level proficiency to lowest.

Remember that even high-level readers may struggle with giving a fluent performance. Remind students that they are performing a play using only their voices. The way they speak each word matters! Demonstrate the difference between monotone reading and reading with fluency and expression so students can understand the expectations.

You might also consider assigning nonspeaking roles to students who are reluctant to read aloud. These students could act as directors or coaches. Remind them that their role is very important. They will have to know the script extremely well and will be in charge of prompting students when it is their turn to read.

Grade 5 Reading Levels:

Narrator 1   Played by: _______________________________

Narrator 2   Played by: _______________________________

Ignatius Donnelly Played by: _______________________________

Grade 4 Reading Levels:

Plato   Played by: _______________________________

Bruce Blackburn   Played by: _______________________________

Tim Akers   Played by: _______________________________

The Lost City Badge Art

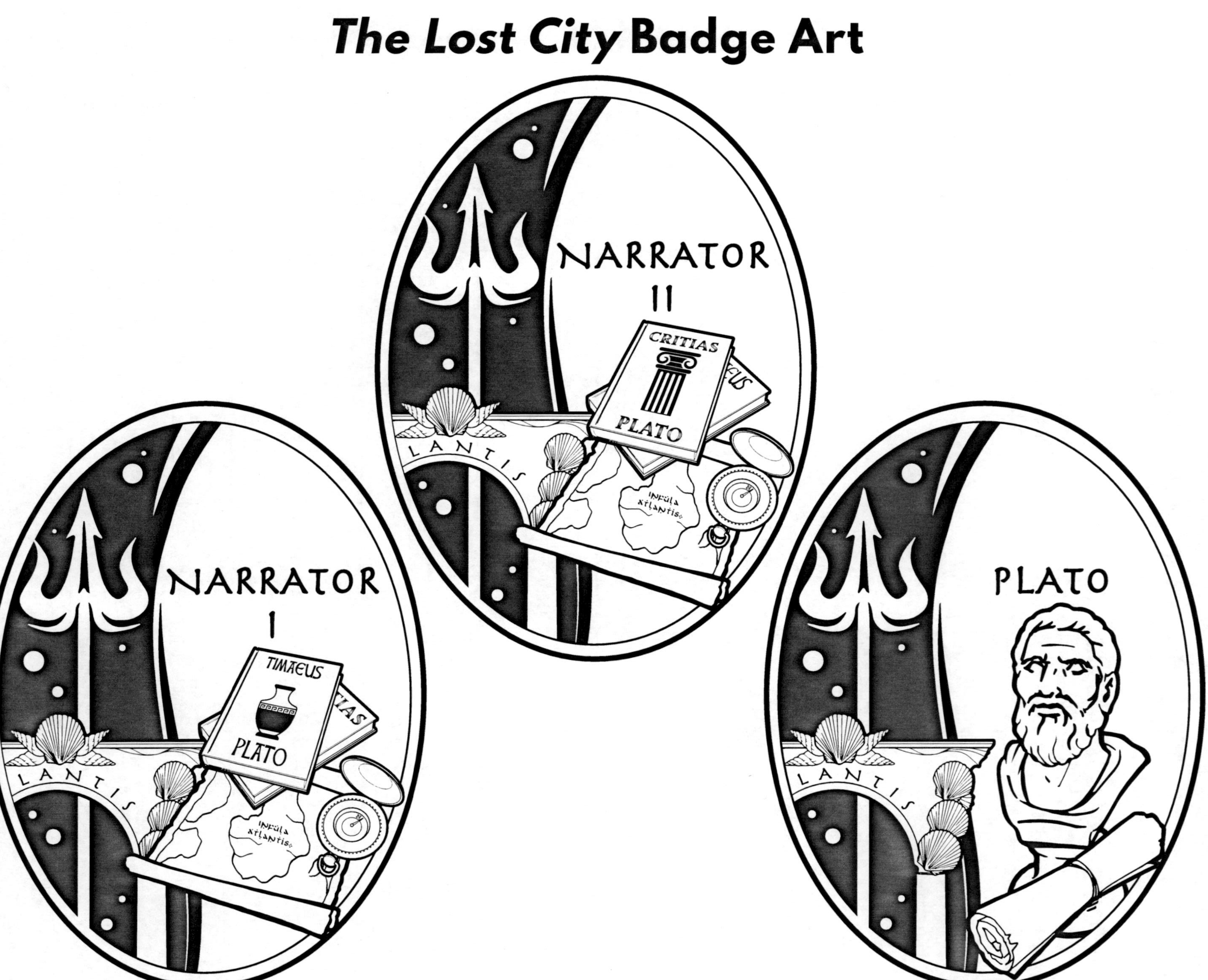

The Lost City Badge Art *(cont.)*

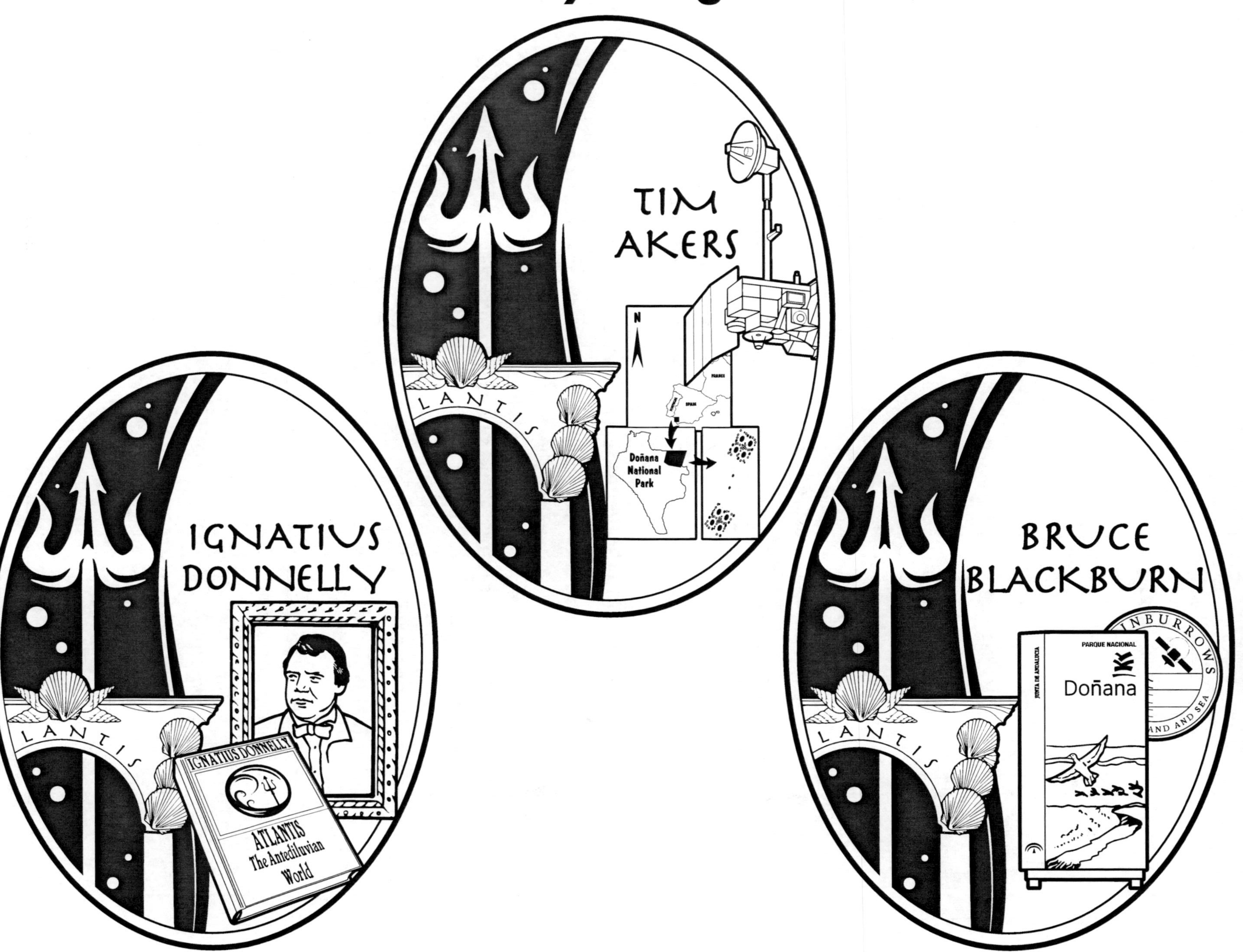

The Lost City

The Lost City Script

Setting

Act 1 takes place in ancient Greece in the 4th century.
Act 2 takes place in 1882 in America. Act 3 takes place
in modern-day Spain.

Act 1

Narrator 1: Plato was an ancient Greek philosopher. He told stories to educate people on how to be good citizens and make wise choices.

Narrator 2: In 360 BCE, Plato told a story. It would create a lasting legend known by many people today. Let's listen to Plato's famous tale.

Plato: Listen closely as I tell the story of Atlantis. Long ago, there was a large and beautiful island. It was in the Atlantic Ocean. It was located beyond the Pillars of Hercules. The soil was rich. Crops grew everywhere throughout the year. Exotic animals roamed freely across the land. It overflowed with precious metals, such as gold and silver.

Narrator 1: Plato described Atlantis as a paradise.

Plato: The god Poseidon fell in love with a mortal who lived on the island. Her name was Cleito. Together they had five sets of twin boys. They were half god, half human. Poseidon wanted to keep his family on the island safe. So, he created the capital city and named it Atlantis. The city was constructed high on a mountaintop. There were three rings of water that surrounded the city. Stone walls were built between the rings of water. These circles protected the city from invaders. A palace and a temple dedicated to Poseidon were at the center of the city.

Narrator 1: The ancient Greeks believed in many gods. Poseidon was the god of the sea.

Narrator 2: Poseidon's oldest son was named Atlas. He was named the first king of Atlantis. The other brothers ruled over the other nine smaller regions on the island.

Plato: At first, the citizens of Atlantis were very happy. They lived in wealth and luxury. Their island provided them with everything they needed. They were prosperous. The people were educated and talented. They built harbors and extensive irrigation systems. They had warm-water bathhouses and gardens. They even invented their own alphabet. Atlantis was the example of a perfect world. There was nothing lacking. The people lived in harmony.

The Lost City Script *(cont.)*

Narrator 1: But there is a moral to this story. Excessive greed leads to misery.

Plato: The island had an abundance of metals and timber. This allowed Atlanteans to build a mighty fleet of ships. Their military was strong. Soon, they conquered lands that ranged from Egypt to Italy. As time progressed, the people relied less on the gods and became greedy. They stopped worshipping Poseidon. One day, they attacked the virtuous land of Athens. The Atlanteans lost the battle, which was most likely because of the power of the gods. Athena, goddess of wisdom and war, protected Athens. That night, the gods assembled. They believed that the people of Atlantis had grown too wicked and selfish. Poseidon delivered storms and earthquakes that shook the city of Atlantis all night. By the next day, Atlantis was swallowed up by the sea and vanished. All that remained was a shoal of mud. It marked the location of the once-perfect paradise of Atlantis.

Narrator 2: Was Plato telling a story simply to provide his audience with a moral? Geologists think an island that size could not be swallowed up by the ocean in just one night.

Narrator 1: Others believe that Plato mixed real history with philosophy. He used real-world events, but created his own moral tales about them. So, perhaps part of the legend is true, and there was an actual city of Atlantis. But if so, where could it be?

Narrator 2: For a thousand years, the legend of Atlantis was only ever mentioned by Plato. There were no other scholars to confirm any truth to his story. The incredible account was fading from popularity.

Act 2

Narrator 1: But in 1882, the story was given new life by author Ignatius Donnelly.

Narrator 2: In addition to being a writer, Ignatius was an American politician. He was a member of the U.S. House of Representatives. He was also a state senator.

Ignatius: My time in the Minnesota Senate is over. I am ready to focus on my writing career. For years, I have been thinking about Plato's writings on Atlantis. I am a believer! I want to share my thoughts with the world. I can give this story new life!

Narrator 1: In 1882, Ignatius wrote a book called *Atlantis: The Antediluvian World*.

The Lost City Script *(cont.)*

Ignatius: I am not only an author and a politician. I am a scientist! I have studied Plato's writings. I believe there are elements of truth to be told. There are ways to link his story to real-world events. For years, different religions and cultures have referenced the Great Flood. What if this flood were the same one that sunk Atlantis? It is possible!

Narrator 2: Ignatius hoped his years of research on Atlantis would spark an interest in the legend of the lost city.

Ignatius: In my book, I show the world how the city of Atlantis was the beginning of all humanity. Plato said that Atlantis was a city 9,000 years before he existed! The description of the tools, buildings, and technology was so far ahead of its time. I believe Atlantis was a special place. It marked humans' entrance into civilization.

Narrator 1: Ignatius studied geography. He tried to pinpoint where Atlantis would fall on a map.

Ignatius: I think the vast island of Atlantis connected the continents of South America and Africa. How else can we explain how produce like bananas was exchanged between those two places? Different cultures across the world had shared knowledge and ideas. I think they all came from Atlantis. Atlantis must be located in the center of it all. Plato speaks of the island being beyond the Pillars of Hercules. I think he means the Strait of Gibraltar. Atlantis is exactly where Plato said. But today it is so far beneath sea level that it is undetectable.

Narrator 1: The Strait of Gibraltar is a channel. It connects the Mediterranean Sea with the Atlantic Ocean.

Ignatius: I think that the modern inventions that we attribute to different countries all came from Atlantis. Consider the modern alphabet. I bet that came from Atlantis. I believe the way the modern world learned to use metals in buildings and architecture came from Atlantis. The city marked the start of it all. But it also gives us hope for what our society and civilization can be once more. I think America can create a utopian society just like Atlantis once was! We can learn from their mistakes. We can be a better nation.

Narrator 2: Ignatius believed that Plato's story was meant to teach a lesson. But he was one of the first scholars to say that the story was based on a real location.

The Lost City Script *(cont.)*

Ignatius: Maybe one day we will have the technology we need to uncover the real lost city of Atlantis. I believe that what Plato wrote about the city sinking under the ocean is possible. But I also think a few people managed to escape. They traveled both east and west. They told people about the destruction of their city. That is how the story reached Plato many years later. I hope the world reads my book about Atlantis and that the spark ignites a fire to investigate the dreamlike world of Atlantis.

Narrator 1: Ignatius's book did exactly what he wanted it to do! The world began talking about the lost city of Atlantis with a renewed interest.

Narrator 2: Scholars and scientists began studying more about Atlantis. Perhaps it really was a beautiful island that sank beneath the ocean.

Act 3

Narrator 1: But then, over the years, the interest in Atlantis fizzled out again. Modern geologists doubted the island could disappear in one day. Even if there was a great flood or the Ice Age raised the sea levels, it seemed unlikely that it could happen that quickly.

Narrator 2: Plato's historians doubted that there was much truth in his tale at all. Plato was a philosopher. He wrote most of his stories for educational purposes only. Why would the tale of Atlantis be any different?

Narrator 1: But modern technology has a way of bringing things to life! In 2018, a company called Merlin Burrows made a new claim. They said they found the lost city of Atlantis. The company says they can find anything that is lost, forgotten, or hidden with great accuracy.

Narrator 2: CEO Bruce Blackburn and researcher Tim Akers told the world that they had made the discovery. But did they really do it? Let's find out.

Bruce: Welcome to this press conference. My name is Bruce Blackburn. I am the head of Merlin Burrows. Our company hires specialists in all areas of expertise. We have historians and archeologists devoted to finding national treasures, lost aircraft and ships, and now, hidden underwater cities! I am here with my head researcher, Mr. Tim Akers. We want to show the world what we have discovered.

The Lost City Script *(cont.)*

Tim: I'd like to begin by explaining what we do. New technology has changed the way we hunt for lost treasure. We have satellites way out in space that orbit Earth. The satellites scan the bottoms of the oceans. Then they return images of what they find. The satellite images can show any abnormal shapes or objects. These are things we could never see from the surface of the water.

Bruce: We usually focus our satellites on certain areas when we are looking for hidden things because we are in search of something. But this time was very unusual! We weren't looking for a specific treasure, but started noticing some strange satellite imagery. The satellites returned images from under the water near Doñana National Park. This is a wetland area in Andalucía, which is located in southern Spain.

Tim: Yes. So as Mr. Blackburn just said, we weren't exactly sure what we were seeing. We just stumbled upon it when studying our images. The satellites showed a huge structure underneath the water. My research team analyzed every single photo. It appeared to be a patterned set of circles. We think these are the bases of ancient towers. Maybe these are the Towers of Poseidon! It also looks as if there is a harbor made by humans built around it. We measured it, and the harbor is over five miles long!

Bruce: We sent out a team of archeologists to Spain to do more research. Our hope was that there were more hidden treasures that would explain the underwater structure.

Tim: When we began searching Doñana National Park and the surrounding areas, we found some amazing things! We found a cave made by humans. It looks like it could be a burial tomb. We found a stone formation that doesn't appear to be Greek or Roman at all. This could be another clue that the Atlantean people lived in this area.

Bruce: Tell them about the patina!

Tim: Oh yes! We found a greenish-blue patina on some of the ruins in this area. A *patina* is a film found on the surface of certain metals that have oxidized over time. When we examined the metals, we found them to be unique combinations. They also date earlier than the Greek or Roman times. The samples showed that the materials are a prehistoric kind of concrete.

The Lost City Script *(cont.)*

Bruce: This proves Plato's assertion that the Atlanteans were a highly advanced civilization. Creating concrete and building these kinds of structures is technology that would not be part of the modern world for many years later.

Tim: We are running tests to prove that the concrete was, in fact, made by people. We have also teamed up with a filmmaker. He is going to make a documentary of our findings. We want to make sure everyone can watch the journey to Atlantis unfold.

Bruce: Stay tuned!

Narrator 1: The world stayed tuned. But nothing more was released, including the documentary.

Narrator 2: It seems that even the high-tech satellite imagery turned out to be mistaken.

Narrator 1: The circles that the Merlin Burrows company discovered under the ocean were most likely not ancient structures from the lost city of Atlantis.

Narrator 2: Archeologists say the circles were actually experimental ponds. They were created in the early 2000s to measure zooplankton.

Narrator 1: So that's it? Atlantis is still a lost city?

Narrator 2: Well, there's always the alien theory. Atlanteans were really aliens with advanced technology. They live under the sea and sometimes fly above the ocean in UFOs.

Narrator 1: Or, the entire city of Atlantis disappeared in the mysterious Bermuda Triangle!

Narrator 2: There is also the theory that Plato was telling a completely made-up story. He only wanted to teach the world a lesson. Great and perfect civilizations can become corrupt. And we will always be subject to the forces of nature!

Narrator 1: There are many possible theories. But one thing unites them all. The lost city of Atlantis will continue to fascinate people as an unsolved mystery. What do *you* think happened?

The Lost City Activity

1. List three things that made Atlantis a paradise.

____

____

2. What is the moral of Plato's story?

____

____

3. How did Ignatius Donnelly reignite the spark in the public's search for Atlantis?

____

____

4. The Merlin Burrows company was certain they discovered Atlantis. What do you think they learned from their research?

____

____

____

Reader's Theater Reflections

Think about your performance. Color in the number of stars to show how well you did in each area.

Accuracy: I read my part correctly.	☆ ☆ ☆
Rate: I read at a pace that was not too fast or too slow.	☆ ☆ ☆
Expression: I read my character's part with feeling and emotion.	☆ ☆ ☆

List one way that you can improve your reader's theater performance.

____

____

The Lost City Journal

Do you think Plato told the story just to teach a lesson? If so, why do you think he made up the city of Atlantis? Or, do you think the city of Atlantis is really lost? If so, do you think it will ever be found? Explain your answer.

The Winchester Mystery House
Lesson Plan

Content Objectives

- Read grade-level text orally with accuracy, appropriate rate, and expression on successive readings.
- Use knowledge of language and its conventions when writing, speaking, reading, or listening.
- Acknowledge differences in the points of view of characters, including by speaking in a different voice for each character when reading dialogue aloud.

Materials

- student copies of *The Winchester Mystery House* Badge Art (pages 103–104)
- student copies of *The Winchester Mystery House* Script (pages 105–110)
- student copies of *The Winchester Mystery House* Activity (page 111)
- student copies of *The Winchester Mystery House* Journal (page 112)
- highlighters, crayons, markers

Before Reading

1. Begin by assessing students' prior knowledge (if any) of the Winchester Mystery House in San Jose, California. Tell students that Sarah Pardee was born in 1839 in Connecticut. She was beautiful and adored by many people. She fell in love with and married William Winchester, who was the heir to the Winchester Repeating Arms Company. They were known for manufacturing rifles. After years of happiness, the couple had a baby daughter named Annie, who tragically died one month later. Soon after, Sarah's beloved William passed away. That same year, her mother also died. Sarah was alone and devastated. She moved to San Jose, California, in search of a new start. She was left with a vast fortune to spend however she pleased. Sarah bought a small farmhouse on a large plot of land. For the next 38 years, she financed round-the-clock construction on the house. It became a giant mansion, but it was very unusual. Sarah directed all of the architecture. Many of the decisions did not make any sense. She had rooms within rooms and doors that opened to nothing and even staircases leading to walls. Her only demand was that the construction never stop. After her death, there were many theories about why she built the strange and mysterious home. Many people thought she was plagued by the spirits of people who died by the Winchester rifles and that she felt guilty. The maze of rooms was meant to confuse the haunted spirits. Others said she just had unusual taste in design. Some people thought she was trying to re-create happy memories from her marriage. Whatever the reason, the house is still a place of mystery. Many people believe it is still haunted!

2. Tell students that they will be performing a reader's theater play about the unsolved mystery of the Winchester Mystery House. Distribute copies of the script. Assign students their roles based on reading proficiencies. See page 102 for a list of the reading levels for each role in *The Winchester Mystery House* script.

The Winchester Mystery House
Lesson Plan *(cont.)*

Rehearsal

1. Once students have been assigned their parts, tell them to go through the entire script and highlight their parts. Then, give students time to silently read either the entire script or just their highlighted sections. Ask them to use a pencil and underline any words that they do not know or do not know how to pronounce. Go over these words together to ensure understanding.

2. This script has key vocabulary that students may not know. Have students write down the following words from the play on a piece of paper: *architect, contractor, arthritis, foreman, reclusive, coincidence, paranormal, philanthropist.* Have students look up the definitions and write them down. Then have them quiz one another to ensure understanding.

3. Give students time to practice their reader's theater. Remind them to speak with fluency, rate, expression, and tone. They need to play the role of the character using just their voices! Demonstrate reading a few lines in a dull, monotonous tone. Then, read the same lines with expression and ask students to explain the difference. Do the same thing with reading pace (read lines too quickly or too slowly), and then demonstrate a proper pace. Finally, whisper lines softly. Then, read them again with a proper volume. Ask students if they understand the differences.

Performance

1. There are a variety of ways for your students to perform *The Winchester Mystery House* reader's theater. See pages 5–8 for performance ideas.

2. Distribute copies of the badges (pages 103–104). Give students time to decorate their character's badge using crayons or markers.

3. Remind students to speak loudly and clearly and with confidence! Encourage them to show emotion and feeling with their voices. Even the narrator can show emotion by reading their part with an authoritative and confident tone! If stage fright or public speaking is an issue for some students, remind them to focus on their lines instead of worrying about the audience. And finally, remind students to take deep breaths, smile, and have fun!

Assessment

1. Distribute student copies of *The Winchester Mystery House* Activity (page 111). Go over the activity sheet together, and then have students complete it independently.

2. Distribute student copies of *The Winchester Mystery House* Journal (page 112). Remind students that the reasons for the construction of the Winchester house still remains an unsolved mystery. Discuss the possible theories presented in the script, along with any of your own. Then, give students time to journal their theories.

The Winchester Mystery House
Characters

Assigning Characters

The roles in this reader's theater have been leveled to fit the individual needs of your students. When students feel confident in their reading fluency, they will engage with the character and feel comfortable performing in front of others. The goal is to have a successful performance that allows each student a chance to shine.

The Winchester Mystery House has six roles. Each role has been designed to meet the needs of a variety of reading-level proficiencies. The characters are listed here in order of highest reading-level proficiency to lowest.

Remember that even high-level readers may struggle with giving a fluent performance. Remind students that they are performing a play using only their voices. The way they speak each word matters! Demonstrate the difference between monotone reading and reading with fluency and expression so students can understand the expectations.

You might also consider assigning nonspeaking roles to students who are reluctant to read aloud. These students could act as directors or coaches. Remind them that their role is very important. They will have to know the script extremely well and will be in charge of prompting students when it is their turn to read.

Grade 5 Reading Levels:

Historian Janan Boehme Played by: _______________________________

Narrator 1 Played by: _______________________________

Narrator 2 Played by: _______________________________

News Reporter Played by: _______________________________

Grade 4/High Grade 3 Reading Levels:

Sarah Winchester Played by: _______________________________

Ranch Foreman John Hansen Played by: _______________________________

The Winchester Mystery House Badge Art

The Winchester Mystery House Badge Art (cont.)

The Winchester Mystery House Script

Characters
- Narrator 1
- Narrator 2
- Sarah Winchester
- Ranch Foreman John Hansen
- News Reporter
- Historian Janan Boehme

Setting

Act 1 takes place in April of 1906 in San Jose, California. Act 2 takes place in the same location but in modern day.

Act 1

Narrator 1: Sarah Pardee was born in 1839. She grew up in Connecticut.

Narrator 2: She fell in love with and married William Winchester. After that, she was known as Sarah Winchester. William's family owned the Winchester Repeating Arms Company. They manufactured rifles.

Narrator 1: Sarah and William had a large income because of the rifle company. Together, they renovated their home and lived happily. They rejoiced when they had their daughter, Annie.

Narrator 2: But sadly, tragedy struck the Winchester family. Baby Annie did not live for more than one month. Sarah also lost her beloved William and then her own mother. She was devastated.

Narrator 1: In 1886, Sarah left the East Coast. She needed a new start. Sarah bought a small farmhouse in San Jose, California. For many years, she lived alone. John Hansen was the ranch foreman. He tended to her property.

Narrator 2: And that is where this unsolved mystery begins.

Sarah: John! Do you have a spare moment today? I know you are busy tending to things on the ranch and in the garden.

John: I have a spare moment, Mrs. Winchester. I have been polishing all of the statues in the garden and watering the plants. The cherry laurels are blooming right now. You should invite some guests over to take a stroll.

Sarah: Not today, John.

John: Very well, Mrs. Winchester. How can I assist you today?

Sarah: I have my daily architectural plans for the new rooms, and I was hoping you could take them to the contractor today.

The Winchester Mystery House Script *(cont.)*

Narrators 1 and 2: [*banging on the floor or wall loudly*]

John: Additional construction? My goodness, will it ever conclude? It's been endless years and years of daily building and rebuilding and constant racket!

Sarah: I sincerely apologize for the loud noises, John, but the work must continue. Now, here are my new plans for the thirteenth bathroom. I want it off the third-story hallway next to the thirteenth bedroom on that floor. I have detailed notes on the thirteen panes of glass that need to be in the bathroom window.

John: [*sighs*] Okay, I will inform the contractor. Will this bathroom finally have a mirror and a shower? Or will it be like the other eleven bathrooms that you had constructed before?

Sarah: Oh, John, you know I have reasons for the way things need to be done around here. But yes, no shower or mirror in that bathroom, please. And remember to tell the workers that the walls need thirteen panels and the staircase to the bathroom needs thirteen steps.

John: There is another new staircase? It's just a bathroom. We can build it off the bedroom if you want, and that will save us the need for another staircase. We already have three elevators. Plus, the staircases are hard on you with your arthritis.

Sarah: I don't question the plans. I simply oversee them and ensure that they get done. Thank you for your advice, but I want a staircase. Please remind them to make the stair steps only two inches tall, so it will be easier for me to climb them. Oh, and remember that they must use redwood, and the stair posts need to be installed upside down.

John: I know, Mrs. Winchester. We will use redwood, but we will paint it whatever color you choose. I know the plain redwood color is not your favorite. We will follow all of your special requests. Do you have any more construction requirements for today?

Sarah: No, that is all for today. Please remind the workers to never stop building! I will bring them more ideas tomorrow.

John: Of course, Mrs. Winchester. I will deliver the new blueprints to the construction manager right away.

Narrator 2: John never asked Sarah who was giving her the ideas for the strange plans or if they were all her own architectural designs.

The Winchester Mystery House Script *(cont.)*

Narrator 1: Sarah ordered daily construction on the house. It began the day she purchased it.

Narrator 2: Whenever she was asked when it would end, Sarah replied that the construction needed to continue. She inherited her husband's company and his fortune. Money was never an issue, so she spent her days hiring more workers.

Narrator 1: The workers often worked in shifts. That way, construction could last 24 hours a day. The pounding of hammers never stopped. That is, until the morning of April 18, 1906.

Narrator 2: Just a little after 5 o'clock in the morning, the earth began violently shaking.

John: Mrs. Winchester, we just had a terrible earthquake! I have come to make sure you are okay. Where are you? What room did you sleep in last night? There are forty bedrooms in this crazy mansion! Why can't you sleep in the same room each night? This is madness!

Narrator 1: Sarah never slept in the same bedroom more than one night. She rotated rooms throughout the house each night at random.

Sarah: John, I am trapped in the Daisy bedroom! The door is stuck, and the walls are falling apart. The entire house sounds like it is crumbling to the ground. All of my years as the architect of my beautiful mansion will be lost!

Narrator 2: John used a crowbar to pry open the room and rescued Sarah.

Sarah: Thank you for saving me, John. I appreciate your service. I know I can always rely on you.

John: Mrs. Winchester, I hate to tell you this, but the earthquake damaged much of the house. You were very lucky to be on this floor. The top three floors collapsed. We will have to stop construction today.

Sarah: No! We cannot stop. This is my mission, and I have to complete it. I cannot stop construction. We can just board up the front rooms that collapsed and continue building. We can build around the fallen rooms. The workers can keep working to repair the damage.

John: Okay, Mrs. Winchester. Let's make sure everyone is unharmed, and then we will have the crews begin reconstruction. I am thankful you are safe.

The Winchester Mystery House Script *(cont.)*

The Winchester Mystery House

Act 2

Narrator 1: Construction did not end until Sarah took her last breath on September 5, 1922.

Narrator 2: Sarah's niece sold all of her aunt's belongings. Sarah's home was opened as a museum for the public to tour a few months after her death.

Narrator 1: Today it is managed by historian Janan Boehme. For years, there have been many theories about the mysterious home.

Narrator 2: Janan offered to do an interview with the press to explain why the home still remains a bit of a mystery.

News Reporter: Good afternoon, Ms. Boehme. Thank you for meeting with me today to discuss the intriguing Winchester Mystery House. Theories have been swirling about why Sarah built the strange mansion. One theory is that she felt haunted by the spirits of the people who died by a Winchester rifle. The maze of construction in the house was meant to throw off the spirits and keep them confused. Do you think she suffered from the guilt of owning a rifle company?

Janan: That theory also says that the spirits were the ones telling her what to build. It is a very popular theory. It is the main reason that tourists continue to visit the house today. I cannot say that Sarah was answering to spirits or ghosts. But I think it is a way for people to try to explain Sarah's peculiar behaviors. No, I do not think that she felt guilt for owning her husband's rifle company. We have a few letters that she wrote that are in a special library at Stanford University. There is never any mention in the letters of her feeling guilty.

News Reporter: Well, I read that Sarah only had two mirrors in the entire house because the spirits were afraid of their reflections. I also heard that she slept in a different room each night to confuse the spirits. How can you explain that?

Janan: Yes, she only had a few mirrors. And yes, she did sleep in a new room each night, but there can be many reasons for that. Honestly, I am not sure what the answer is for that. I don't think anyone ever asked her.

News Reporter: What about reports that the house is still haunted? Multiple workers have claimed to see ghosts! Have you ever seen a ghost in the house?

The Winchester Mystery House Script *(cont.)*

Janan: You are right. The Winchester Mystery House ranks high on the list of paranormal activity. But no, I have never seen a ghost there. There are rumors of certain spooky things like strange noises in the night. Other witnesses say they saw moving lights or doorknobs that turned on their own. Multiple visitors say they have seen a ghost repairing a fireplace. He has a mustache and pushes a wheelbarrow. But no, I have never seen him.

News Reporter: So, you don't believe Sarah was constantly constructing the house to ward off ghosts? What other reason explains the need for 24 hours a day of hammering?

Janan: Sarah did not have any friends. She stayed home alone for most of her life. She only spoke to her niece or to the people who worked for her. That being said, she had a great social conscience. She wanted to give back to the community. Sarah paid her workers three times the going rate. No one ever complained about having a construction job at the Winchester House. So, my theory is that she was merely a great philanthropist.

News Reporter: That is a possibility. But why did she design such random construction? There are staircases that lead to nowhere. There are rooms built within rooms. There are even doors that open into nothing!

Janan: The house itself is truly a mystery. When Sarah purchased the home, it only had six rooms. She was the only architect to oversee all of the construction. Under her plans, the house grew into a sprawling mansion with 161 rooms. There were 40 bedrooms and 13 bathrooms. She added 47 fireplaces, elevators, and multiple staircases. And yes, there are some unusual designs. Some people claim it's because she was trying to trick the ghosts that were haunting her. I am not sure that was the reason.

News Reporter: How do you explain the senseless designs and odd behavior? I mean, there are chimneys in the house that stop midway up the wall and others that aren't even attached to fireplaces. Was Sarah mentally ill?

Janan: Honestly, I do not think she was at all. I believe the strange architecture can be explained in other ways. I think Sarah was trying to repeat the experiences she had with her late husband. They renovated their first home together. I think the construction helped her remember doing something they both loved.

News Reporter: I love that theory. But what about her reclusive behavior? Even if the house wasn't haunted, there was a mysterious quality about her.

The Winchester Mystery House Script *(cont.)*

Janan: There was, but she wasn't always that way. Sarah was the center of society in Connecticut. She was beautiful and surrounded by friends. But tragedy made her withdraw. She moved to a new place and never became part of society in San Jose. Plus, she had health problems. Her arthritis made it hard for her to get around. I also think she became too obsessed with the construction. I have studied her letters, and she admitted that her designs got weirder over the years. One of her letters read, "This house looks like it was built by a crazy person." So, Sarah was definitely aware of what it looked like. After the earthquake, so much of the house was boarded up. Rooms that were unsafe were just built around. It is a strange maze of a place.

News Reporter: Thank you, Ms. Boehme, for your time. I have one last question for you. Has anything ever happened that you found to be paranormal at all? Or do you really believe there is nothing haunted or mysterious about the Winchester House?

Janan: For years, I worked at the house without ever thinking there was anything out of the ordinary. I mean, other than the weird architecture and design. But I did have one very unusual experience that I will never forget. We had an architect visit the home because he was curious about the stained-glass windows. We never knew who made them, and they truly are quite beautiful. We studied the design closely, but we didn't know how to prove which artist actually created the windows. I was feeling discouraged that I didn't have the answer. Then, the very next day, the strangest thing happened. I had a team of workers renovating one of the rooms. They had just removed a portion of the wall and found an envelope. They gave it to me. Imagine my surprise when I opened it and found a photo of a stained-glass window and the logo of the Pacific American Decorative Company! It was as if Sarah wanted to answer my question.

News Reporter: Ms. Boehme, that does not sound like just a coincidence! It sounds to me like a ghost was trying to help you out. I am sure Sarah was very proud of the mysterious and beautiful mansion she created. Thank you for your expertise.

Narrator 1: Nobody knows exactly why Sarah was compelled to construct the strange home. But it remains open for visitors to tour today.

Narrator 2: Do you think Sarah built the mansion to confuse the ghosts that haunted her? Or was she just trying out her own architectural ideas? Why did the construction need to be constant?

Narrator 1: Is the Winchester Mystery house really haunted? Or was Sarah just trying to re-create some of the happy memories from her past? What do *you* think?

The Winchester Mystery House
Activity

1. Why did Sarah move to California?

____

____

2. How did much of the house get destroyed in 1906?

____

3. Why do people think the house is haunted?

____

____

4. Why do you think Sarah wanted constant construction on her house?

____

____

____

Reader's Theater Reflections

Think about your performance. Color in the number of stars to show how well
you did in each area.

Accuracy: I read my part correctly.	☆ ☆ ☆
Rate: I read at a pace that was not too fast or too slow.	☆ ☆ ☆
Expression: I read my character's part with feeling and emotion.	☆ ☆ ☆

List one way that you can improve your reader's theater performance.

____

The Winchester Mystery House
Journal

There are many unsolved mysteries when it comes to the Winchester Mystery House. Is the house really haunted? Why did Sarah construct it the way she did? What do you think?